TURN ME ON

TURN ME ON

100 EASY WAYS
TO USE SOLAR ENERGY

Michelle Kodis

GIBBS SMITH
TO ENRICH AND INSPIRE HUMANKIND
Salt Lake City | Charleston | Santa Fe | Santa Barbara

First Edition
13 12 11 10 09   10 9 8 7 6 5 4 3 2 1

Published by
Gibbs Smith
P.O. Box 667
Layton, Utah 84041

1.800.835.4993 orders
www.gibbs-smith.com

Designed and produced by Linda Herman, Glyph Publishing Arts
Printed and bound in Canada
Gibbs Smith books are printed on either recycled, 100% post-consumer waste, FSC-certified papers or on paper produced from a 100% certified sustainable forest/controlled wood source.

Library of Congress Cataloging-in-Publication Data

Kodis, Michelle.
    Turn me on : 100 easy ways to use solar energy / Michelle Kodis. — 1st ed.
        p. cm.
    ISBN-13: 978-1-4236-0519-5
    ISBN-10: 1-4236-0519-5
    1. Solar energy. I. Title.
    TJ810.K58 2009
    621.47—dc22
                                        2009000068

For Rich, the sunshine of my life

ACKNOWLEDGMENTS

My deepest appreciation and gratitude to: Suzanne Taylor, Michelle Witte, Gibbs Smith, Christopher Robbins, Hollie Keith, Madge Baird, Bob and Joan Kodis, Rosemerry, Kendall, Anne, Maureen, Kierstin, Pam, Marcia, Andrew, Brett, Violet, and Renzo.

CONTENTS

INTRODUCTION

Each month, those of us who live "on the grid" get a little gift in the mail: an invoice for our electricity usage. Prior to that bill arriving, the little meter attached to our homes has been spinning day and night, tallying our energy use as we power up our computers, stuff our wet towels into the dryer, forget to turn off the lights when we leave a room, pop in a DVD, fire up the coffee-maker, and so on. Our debt to the power company can fluctuate depending on the season. In winter, of course, we can't do without that toasty electric blanket, right? When indeed the bill is higher in the winter months, we sigh, thinking that we really should start finding ways to reduce our fossil fuel consumption and do our part for the planet—but it all seems so . . . complex and time-consuming, and we don't know where to start. We write the check and it's on to next month. *Click. Click. Click.* That's the sound of the meter costing you money. Ready to learn about a new way? Read on.

Currently, the United States is a fossil fuel–dependent nation. We could not function without the grid, the intricate and vast network of electrical utility distribution. When you hear about a person who lives "off the grid," this means he or she has either fully or partially ended dependence on the grid for energy by substituting alternative means of generating power. While *Turn Me On* does not aim to get you grid-independent by early next week, we do hope it will provide the inspiration and impetus to learn more about the ways—some of them very, very easy and very, very free—to end total reliance on diminishing fossil fuels.

I wholeheartedly thank and salute you for choosing this book. In doing so, you have joined an unstoppable global movement that is transforming, at seemingly warp speed, how we view the inherent limitations of our precious natural resources. That movement is giving us intelligent and innovative new choices for how we conduct our lives. Maybe you already know a thing or two about solar power, or perhaps you've chosen this book to begin building a knowledge base to get you started on a more in-depth path toward renewable energy. Whatever your individual experience or goal, I hope *Turn Me On* helps you develop a passion for solar power that you will pass on to others.

As the third title in Gibbs Smith's series of "eco" handbooks (the first two, *It's Easy Being Green* and *Go Green,* have enjoyed much-deserved success), *Turn Me On* is a lively and educational glimpse at all things solar. In these pages, you'll find everything from descriptions about the latest and greatest technology to how to use a simple solar oven. From the outset, my goal in compiling this body of information was to give you as many ideas and tidbits for thought as possible without overwhelming you with too much technical detail and data. My guess is that after reading *Turn Me On* you'll be craving a deeper understanding of both technology and policy, and you'll find plenty of additional reading suggestions in these pages.

Turn Me On does not have a fancy table of contents or clever organizational tactics. It is a straightforward, sequential, 1 to 100 journey of ideas, insights, technology, science, collaboration, inspiration, surprises, guidance, and, even, pop culture. And, it has been designed to guide you through the information as effortlessly as possible; for that I am indebted to the talented graphic designer, Linda Herman, who took my words and shaped them into a cohesive book that I hope will have a positive influence on your life, and on the lives of those around you.

The snappy title, courtesy of Gibbs Smith vice president and editorial director, Suzanne Taylor, and the cheerful art on the cover and throughout the text, clearly indicate that we are having some fun with this topic. We're not going to go into any heavy detail. We promise you we won't get pedantic or pushy. This handbook is a springboard. Use it, share it, add to it using the blank journal pages at the end of the book. Here's the deal, folks: environmentalism does not have to be a heart-heavy endeavor in which the constant reminder of a planet in peril permeates our collective daily mood. Quite the opposite. There is great hope to be had as this book enters the marketplace. Across the world, great thinkers, innovators, and leaders are searching for and discovering ways to shift to clean, renewable energy. Every day, it seems, a new development or trend in sustainability and alternative energy arrives, reminding us to always look on the bright side of things.

—Michelle Kodis

SHOULD YOU CARE ABOUT CARBON?

The following essay, "Why Carbon Matters," is courtesy of Carbon Monitoring for Action (CARMA), **www.carma.org.** Through its massive database of information on the carbon emissions of more than 50,000 power plants and 4,000 power companies worldwide, CARMA aims to equip individuals with the information they need to forge a cleaner, low-carbon future. CARMA is produced and financed by the Confronting Climate Change Initiative at the Center for Global Development, an independent and non-partisan think tank located in Washington, D.C. This essay is an excellent explanation of why renewable energy sources are more crucial than ever to the sustained health of the planet. (This essay is reprinted with permission from the Center for Global Development, **www.cgdev.org** / **www.carma.org.**)

The bulk of humanity's energy needs are currently met through the combustion of fossil fuels like coal, oil, and natural gas. About 60 percent of global electricity generation relies upon fossil fuels to make the heat needed to power steam-driven turbines. Burning these fuels results in the production of carbon dioxide (CO_2)—the primary heat-trapping "greenhouse gas" responsible for global warming.

If our greenhouse gas emissions succeed in pushing the climate past the point of no return, we are unlikely to realize it until it is too late to avoid the consequences.

Over the past two centuries, mankind has increased the concentration of CO_2 in the atmosphere from 280 to more than 380 parts per million volume, and it is growing faster every day. The atmospheric concentration of CO_2 has not been this high for at least the past 650,000 years. As the concentration of CO_2

has risen, so has the average temperature of the planet. Over the past century, the average surface temperature of Earth has increased by more than 1.3°F (0.74°C). If we continue to emit carbon without restraint, temperatures are expected to rise by an additional 6°F (3.4°C) by the end of this century.

Climate change of that magnitude would likely have serious consequences for life on Earth. Sea level rise, droughts, floods, intense storms, forest fires, water scarcity, and cardio-respiratory and tropical diseases would be exacerbated. Agricultural systems would be stressed—possibly decimated in some parts of the world. A conservative estimate suggests that 30 percent of all species are at risk of extinction given current trends. It would be the greatest extinction of life on Earth since the K-T extinction event that destroyed the dinosaurs 65 million years ago. No one can imagine—never mind predict—the ecological consequences of such a radical loss of life.

Mankind probably needs to reduce total CO_2 emissions by at least 80 percent by 2050.

There is also the risk that continued warming will push the planet past critical thresholds or "tipping points"—like the large-scale melting of polar ice, the thawing of tundra or methane clathrates, the collapse of the Amazon rain forest, or the warming and acidification of the oceans—that will make further climate change inescapable and irreversible. The history of Earth suggests that such positive feedback loops in the climate system are powerful and often severe. If our greenhouse gas emissions succeed in pushing the climate past the point of no return, we are unlikely to realize it until it is too late to avoid the consequences.

Despite mounting evidence of the dangers posed by climate change, efforts to limit carbon emissions remain insufficient, ineffective, and, in most countries, non-existent. If the world is to avert the worst consequences of an altered climate, the status quo must change quickly. Given current trends and the best available scientific evidence, mankind probably needs to reduce total CO_2 emissions by at least 80 percent by 2050. Yet each day emissions continue to grow.

In the absence of action on the part of governments, hundreds of millions of increasingly climate-conscious citizens can promote low-carbon alternatives by changing the ways they purchase, invest, vote, think, and live. All you need to act is timely, accurate, publicly available information about the choices you face. It's time to take matters into your own hands.

In the absence of action on the part of governments, hundreds of millions of increasingly climate-conscious citizens can promote low-carbon alternatives by changing the ways they purchase, invest, vote, think, and live.

2
THIS AIN'T YOUR GRANDMA'S SOLAR

In one corner, we have the Sun. In the other corner, the collective "us," otherwise known as the people of the world. We need electricity for myriad reasons. The Sun can provide that energy. What, then, is the formula?

In its essence, the sunshine-to-electricity conversion is not complicated. You have solar radiance (sunlight). That sunlight is collected by silicon photovoltaic (PV) cells. As sunlight hits the cells, electrons are set free, producing electricity. A group of PV cells is called a PV module. The module produces direct current (DC), again, via those free-wheeling electrons. But, DC likely won't work in your home. Why? Because your home is set up for alternating current (AC). This is where the inverter comes in: its job is to convert DC to AC. If you don't need the electricity right away, you can store it in a battery, for later use or on overcast days when the module is not performing at its optimal level. The battery also gives a grid-tied home a backup in the event of a power outage. In addition, charge controllers are necessary for regulating voltage and current moving from the PV module to the battery, preventing damage to the battery from overcharging.

Think of it this way: **PV modules** (harness the energy of sunlight)→**Charge controller** (regulates voltage, prevents battery from overcharging)→**Battery** (stores electricity for later use)→**Inverter** (converts DC to AC)→**End Result:** electricity flowing into the home.

ACTIVELY SOLAR

Active solar is exactly what it sounds like: an actively working solar cell or panel array that uses a series of controls and pumps designed to harness the sun's energy to power your home and heat water.

QUICK TIP

- Protect your PV array's storage battery from over-charging with a charge controller, also called a regulator. The charge controller controls the flow of current to and from the battery and can also monitor overall system performance.

SOLAR QUERIES

4

Here are answers to a few questions you might have about solar.

Why is solar power getting so much attention lately?
It's all about the word "renewable." Unlike power generated by
limited and quickly depleting natural resources (fossil fuels), solar
energy is boundless. The sun produces clean energy without creating the pollutants that contribute to climate change.

**But wait—doesn't the manufacturing of photovoltaics cause
pollution, too?**
Yes, the production of PV cells does create emissions, but studies
show that solar produces less than 15 percent of the carbon
dioxide from a traditional coal-fired power plant. According to
the Environmental Protection Agency, a million homes converted to
solar would reduce carbon dioxide emissions by 4.3 million tons
per year, which is roughly equal to taking 850,000 cars off the road.

Do I need a certain type of house in order to convert to solar?
No, not necessarily. A broad south-facing roof would nicely
accommodate solar panels—if your neighborhood design rules
permit this (make sure you contact your local building department before you embark on a solar retrofit). Photovoltaic panels
can be installed as freestanding arrays if the configuration of
your house doesn't work for solar. New homes have the advantage in that solar rooftop materials can be built directly into the
structure. The reality is this: solar technology is advancing
rapidly, which is good news for consumers because the ways
in which solar can be installed are expanding.

Will I really see savings in my utility bills?
In a word, yes. Solar energy systems can significantly lower your
monthly utility bill. Here's something else you may not have

considered: PV panels will shade your roof by bouncing back all that heat that otherwise would be absorbed and thus increase indoor air temperatures. When you keep your rooms at a nice, cool temperature in the summer, the need for air-conditioning is greatly reduced.

Should I expect to replace my solar array often? I can't afford to do that!

No! The beauty of PV technology is that the panels are designed to last a very long time, depending on levels of active use (most systems are in use for no more than eight hours per day, more likely less) and how much sunshine is being converted into electricity by the individual cells. Most manufacturers provide long-term warranties of 10–20 years, but a solar installer will tell you that the panels will probably outlive the warranty.

Will I have to spend every weekend maintaining my PV array?

Again, no. Because it has no moving parts, a PV system is straightforward and pretty much maintenance-free. If you have a grid-connected array, you will be required to keep the panels clean and clear of debris.

SOLAR GIZMOS

- Interested in an outdoor shower? For about $20, you can purchase a Super Solar Shower. Place it in direct sun on a 70-degree day and it will heat five gallons of water from 60 degrees to 108 degrees.

- Wilting under the hot sun? Need a soothing breeze to cool you off? The Solar Hat Fan is ready for rescue. The small fan is designed to clamp onto a hat, and it begins to spin as the unit's tiny photovoltaic panel soaks up the sun's rays. At only $10 each, consider buying a bunch to give as gifts.

5

SOAK UP THOSE RAYS

It sounds, well, a bit of a snooze-fest, but passive solar energy can be put to good active use. Radiant heat from the sun can be manipulated and controlled to heat and cool interiors, in the process reducing energy consumption and resulting in an energy-efficient dwelling and less money spent on the power company.

The three approaches to a passive setup are **direct gain** (interiors soak up and store sunlight, release heat at night), **indirect gain** (thermal storage wall systems, roof ponds), and **isolate gain** (sunroom, convective loop through air collector, then heat is stored in-house). Your mission? To capture that precious solar warmth within the building and then release it when the sun is behind clouds or at night.

A few basic things to consider:

1. To ensure the most successful passive solar design, choose a site with plenty of solar exposure. Sound obvious? Perhaps, but this main point can sometimes be forgotten in the heady excitement of design and construction. Avoid wooded lots, and be aware of any trees whose growth may eventually impede your home's passive solar capabilities.

2. Orient and lengthen the building along an east–west axis. This ensures plenty of solar-friendly southern exposure. Also, make sure that southern exposure provides at least six hours of powerful sunlight during the cooler months.

3. For solar heating, place the bulk of the glazing on the south-facing facade.

4. Overhangs are crucial to helping control the temperature inside the house. Solar experts in the *Real Goods Solar Living Source Book* explain, "Overhangs on the south side are the on-off switches of a passive solar house." Unless you want to roast in your living room, don't forget the overhangs.

5. You'll find many online sources of information about passive solar. I was helped in my efforts with "A Sourcebook for Green and Sustainable Building," published by the fantastic **www.greenbuilder.com,** a website you should bookmark and get to know in detail. Also, the *Real Goods* solar book described earlier includes a detailed section on the topic, as does *The Complete Idiot's Guide to Solar Power for Your Home*. Both sources include illustrations that nicely demonstrate the concepts at hand.

6. According to the *Idiot's* book, a sunroom is an excellent investment in eco-living and quality of life. Authors Ramsey and Hughes point out: "A well-designed sunspace can provide up to 60 percent of a home's winter heating requirements. In addition, it can offer overnight warmth, summer cooling, and a great place to stretch out and read a book by natural light." Well said!

GET PV'D

Photovoltaics (PV) convert sunlight into electricity. How does this work, exactly? The naturally occurring photons in sunlight represent energy. A solar cell or panel absorbs these photons, at which point a crucial meeting of the minds occurs: the photons interact with the electrons stored in the PV material, exciting and agitating the electrons until the electrons break free to form a current. These free-wheeling electrons need a place to go, so they are directed to batteries for storage for later use, or directed into the building that houses the PV panels for immediate use in powering appliances and other items that require electricity.

WHAT'S YOUR TYPE?

Solar cells, also called PV cells, are small, semi-conducting elements designed to convert sunlight into a "direct current" form of electrical energy. Solar cells wired together form a PV module. The size of a PV module is determined by available sunlight and how much electricity is needed, on a case-by-case basis. The basic types of solar cells are:

Monocrystalline/Single Crystal Silicon: The most widely used. Also tend to be more expensive than other kinds.

Polycrystalline: Less costly than single-crystal silicon cells but not the most efficient when it comes to converting energy.

Amorphous: Widely available and relatively less expensive to produce. They are "without" shape, which means that their silicon is not crystallized or highly structured.

8

ENLIGHTEN ME

Solar panels can be used to:
1. Convert sunlight into electricity via solar cells set on PV modules.
2. Heat water, oil, or antifreeze via solar thermal collectors.

When choosing your solar panels, keep the following in mind:

Cost: How many do you need? How durable are they? Will they need to be replaced soon? Factor maintenance into general cost calculations.

Type: If you want to go solar on a camping trip, you likely won't need the same type of solar panel as you would for residential use. Research solar panels by use; in other words, which are best suited to the task at hand?

Size: Maximum wattage is determined by the size of the panel, as well as the type of solar cells used for the panel. The larger the panel, the more electrical output it has.

Longevity: A good solar installer will direct you toward the options that best fit your needs and budget. Different types of solar cells have different life spans, so pick the one with the longest life span that you can afford. How the panels are framed can make a big difference, too. For example, lightweight and durable aluminum is a popular framing material for solar arrays.

9

FORM AN ATTACHMENT

Solar panels can be attached to your home or arranged in a "free-standing" configuration set apart from the building. Where you ultimately decide to place your PV array will depend on a number of factors, including:

* your neighborhood and its particular set of design rules, which likely will dictate how solar panels can be presented on a building;
* local topography and the immediate landscape around your home. For example, if your home is surrounded by tall trees that block sunlight, you would be advised to place your PV array in a sunny location away from the house;
* building restrictions, such as an architectural design that precludes the placement of roof-mount solar panels on the house;
* personal taste: maybe you love the idea of using the sun to power your home, but you don't necessarily want to see PV panels as you drive up to the front door (there are other solutions to this challenge, such as solar shingles and other new technologies, discussed later in the book).

Your solar installer will make the best recommendation based on your needs and, of course, budget.

EMPOWERED CO-DEPENDENCY

If you're not yet ready to exert your energy independence by going "off the grid," then a grid-tied solar power system could be the right choice. Grid-tied systems essentially act as adjunct power supplies; they augment the electricity coming into your home from the local power company.

Grid-tied folks can enjoy the financial benefits of net metering, a government incentive program that encourages the use of renewables by allowing individual and business consumers who generate excess electricity via non–fossil fuel sources such as solar and wind to "sell" that power back to the local utility in the form of a retail credit. Although net metering rules tend to vary by state, the Energy Policy Act of 2005 mandated that all public electric utilities offer net metering to their customers.

> ### Homeowners feel pride in their eco-friendly contribution. In their experience of creating and using renewable power, they are *empowered*.

So, on sunny days, when a single household does not require all of the power it's generating via its PV panels, the owner of that household can sell this excess electricity back to his power company. On cloudy days, and at night, the household will use power from the grid. The end result is that the consumer's utility costs are calculated on his net electricity usage.

The thrill goes beyond saving money, though. Homeowners who partake in such programs speak of feeling more aware of their overall energy use, and on average they tend to use less energy, thanks to this heightened knowledge. They feel pride in their eco-friendly contribution. In their experience of creating and using renewable power, they are empowered.

The downside? Let's say the grid is down due to inclement weather. That means you are without electricity. Unless you . . .

ALWAYS HAVE A BACKUP

Essentially a more sophisticated (and more expensive) version of the basic grid-tied PV system, the grid-tied battery backup option protects you if the grid is down. How? It's actually quite simple: the inverter that converts direct current (DC) to usable alternating current (AC) is connected to a battery, which is charged by the solar panels. If grid-fed power suddenly stops, the inverter automatically disconnects from the grid and begins to draw power from the charged battery. Voilà! You have backup power!

12 GOING ALL THE WAY

Okay. You've taken the time to educate yourself about renewable energy generated by solar panels. You have taken a deep breath (or two, perhaps three). You are ready to sever all ties to the utility company. You are going *off-grid*.

Off-grid is exactly that: any power coming into your home to power appliances is generated solely by your solar panel array. A backup generator is recommended in case of emergency and to make up for power lost to overcast days.

YES YOU CAN

- If you feel you can't afford to install a solar package in your home, think again: many solar vendors offer financing to help pay for your new system. Take the time to shop for the products with the best interest rates.

13

DELIVERING POWER

You're probably already familiar with this technology: the ability to run your computer when a lightning strike takes out the grid, for example. An uninterruptible power supply (UPS) employs a battery to provide extra run time for appliances in the event of a power outage. Consider a UPS if you can't afford downtime (for example, you work at home) or if you use electricity-powered medical equipment.

INVERT ME, BABY

Without an inverter, the electrical energy collected by your PV system will remain in an unusable form. Inverters convert low-voltage direct current power (DC), which originates at the array or is stored in the battery, to high-voltage alternating current (AC), the electrical power accessible through any standard wall socket. The DC-to-AC conversion automatically results in a loss of power, but this can be mitigated by taking time to find an inverter with a rated efficiency score of 90 percent or more.

Also crucial: ensuring that your inverter's output power matches the maximum wattage capacity of your solar panel or array.

A full discussion of solar inverters is beyond the scope of this book, but you can find plenty of information online and from solar suppliers. Don't be hesitant to ask solar installers which inverters they prefer, and inquire about customer testimonials.

CHARGE IT!

If you want to hang on to all that delicious DC electricity your solar panels are soaking up, you will need a battery. Lead-acid deep cycle batteries, the most commonly used in PV arrays, are designed specially to handle the vagaries of the weather—for example, one day with full sunshine followed by a day with overcast skies and the subsequent charging and discharging that occurs as energy needs wax and wane.

Although lead-acid batteries are more expensive than conventional batteries (such as those used in cars) they do boast a longer shelf life. The key to an optimally performing solar array is a battery ideally matched to the system. In other words, if you choose a battery that is too small to accommodate your system, it will likely discharge too often and require sooner-than-normal replacement. Expect your lead-acid battery to last a good dozen years, if cared for properly.

Battery capacity is measured in ampere-hours (Ah). Individual battery cells contained in the unit store electrical energy channeled in from solar panels. For maximum storage of power, your solar installer might recommend a battery bank: several batteries wired together. The benefits of a battery bank are clear: collected energy is stored for use on overcast days and at night, and should your household require more power than your array is producing at any given moment, the battery backup can be called upon to meet higher energy needs.

You can extend the life of your battery by doing the following: (Thanks to **www.solarguide.com** for this battery-saving to-do list)

* Fully charge the battery before use.
* Tighten the connectors.
* Tightly fasten the vent caps.
* Check the battery regularly for signs of corrosion, and, if present, remove the corrosion, as well as any accumulated dirt and dust.
* Water the battery after extended charging and check the acid level after charging.
* Avoid filling or overfilling the cells: as the battery charges, electrolyte matter can overflow, resulting in corrosion and shortening the life of the battery.
* Use distilled water.

TAKE CHARGE

Without a charge controller, you might as well kiss your battery good-bye—and plan to spend your hard-earned cash replacing it with a new one, and then another one, and . . . well, you get the picture.

The charge controller's job is to protect the battery from taking in too much charge and losing too much charge. An out-of-control battery that overcharges and over-discharges is a battery not long for this world. The charge controller, which is placed between the solar panel(s) and the battery/battery bank, ensures a consistent and maximum charge. This even-keeled state of existence will also extend the life of the battery.

17

ENVIRONMENTAL STEWARD: BARACK OBAMA

"We will harness the sun and the winds and the soil to fuel our cars and run our factories . . ."

—President Barack Obama, inaugural speech, January 20, 2009

The election of Barack Obama as the 44th president of the United States sent up a collective cheer of hope and relief from environmentalists around the world. President Obama has pledged to focus on issues of renewable energy and conservation, and the timing could not be better.

Here are a few highlights from the comprehensive Obama/Biden energy plan:

* Provide short-term relief to American families facing pain at the pump.
* Help create 5 million new jobs by strategically investing $150 billion over the next 10 years to catalyze private efforts to build a clean energy future.
* Within 10 years save more oil than is currently imported from the Middle East and Venezuela combined.

* Put 1 million plug-in hybrid cars—which can get up to 150 miles per gallon—on the road by 2015, cars that they will work to make sure are built in America.
* Ensure 10 percent of electricity comes from renewable sources by 2012, and 25 percent by 2025.
* Implement an economy-wide cap-and-trade program to reduce greenhouse gas emissions 80 percent by 2050.
* Enact a Windfall Profits Tax to provide a $1,000 Emergency Energy Rebate to American families.
* Crack down on excessive energy speculation.
* Swap oil from the Strategic Petroleum Reserve to cut prices.
* Eliminate current imports from the Middle East and Venezuela within 10 years.
* Increase fuel economy standards.
* Create a new $7,000 tax credit for purchasing advanced vehicles.
* Establish a national low-carbon-fuel standard.
* A "Use It or Lose It" approach to existing oil and gas leases.
* Promote the responsible domestic production of oil and natural gas.
* Weatherize 1 million homes annually.
* Develop and deploy clean coal technology.

18

THE COLD HARD FACTS ABOUT COAL

Big Coal: The Dirty Secret Behind America's Energy Future should be mandatory reading. Its warnings about the dire consequences of a national reliance on coal reads like a horror-flick marquee: "Each American uses approximately 20 pounds of coal each day to fuel our power-hungry life"; "Coal-fired power plants account for 40 percent of the carbon dioxide emissions into the atmosphere"; and "In just the past 20 years, air pollution from coal plants has killed more than half a million Americans." You get the picture. In his groundbreaking book, Goodell makes it clear what will happen if we don't get a handle on our coal-devouring ways. Get a copy. Read it. Be forever changed.

GROWTH SPURTS

The market research firm NanoMarkets projects significant revenue growth for thin-film photovoltaics manufacturers in the coming years. Studies on PV markets reveal an enormous anticipated increase, from the $2.4 billion in estimated 2008 revenues to more than $12 billion in 2013. In addition, the market is set to double by 2015, to some $22 billion.

20 SIZZLING SOLAR JOBS

Industrial Machinery Mechanic
9 percent projected growth
$42,350 median annual income

Someone has to install solar panels and repair wind turbines, and industrial machinery mechanics are often the ones who get the jobs. In solar, Tioga Energy's executive vice president Preston Roper said the biggest demand is for solar installers.

Local community colleges are the places to get training necessary for the jobs. Many are offering specialized training in solar or wind repair work.

21 GET YOUR COMPONENTS IN ORDER

If you're ready to purchase a solar power system for your home, the process will inevitably be easier to navigate if you choose a pre-designed solar package or hire a specialized supplier or contractor.

As Dan Ramsey points out in his brilliant book, *The Complete Idiot's Guide to Solar Power for your Home*, "There's no such thing as a typical photovoltaic system, which is a complete set of components for converting sunlight into electricity by the photovoltaic process, including the array and balance of system components."

Well said, Dan. He goes on to list the common components of any PV system. Smaller systems will not have all the components; the larger ones will. Some of these we've already discussed.

Why not dedicate a special notebook to your solar project? Start it off by listing these solar system components. And, should you want considerably more detail on this subject than this introductory guide offers, definitely invest in Ramsey's excellent book.

SYSTEM COMPONENTS:

* **PV modules**: take sunlight, make electricity.
* **Mounting**: Supports PV modules on a building or on a free-standing array. Orients modules toward sun.
* **Combiner/fusing**: Combines and protects module output wiring.
* **Inverter**: Converts DC to usable AC.
* **Batteries**: Store DC electricity.
* **Charge Controller**: Regulates battery charge and prevents over- and under-charging.
* **Monitor/metering**: Reports system status (current and cumulative) and system flows.
* **Generator**: Provides backup AC power.
* **Power Center**: Encloses controller, overcurrent protection, and monitors in one location.
* **Wiring**: Connects components, allowing flow of electricity.
* **Breakers/Fuses**: Protect against electrical overload.

22 MISS CALCULATION

Each solar array has its own set of particulars, among them budget, location, and individual energy needs. Here are a few useful tips for determining the size of your PV system:

Your geographic location: some locales are sunnier than others. Areas with high numbers of sunny days per year will give you more bang for your solar buck. Maps and charts are available to help you determine average hours of full sun per day, per season.

Professional solar installers use solar calculators to determine energy needs. However, it's unreasonable to expect to calculate a single, set-in-stone number. Be willing to be flexible, and take into consideration the following: Do you want a solar system to provide the bulk of your energy needs, or a partial sum? Is the PV array for a weekend house, versus a full-time dwelling? How do your energy usage trends vary from season to season? Do you use your appliances more frequently during certain parts of the day or week?

Your energy needs will be described in watt hours, watts, or kilowatt hours (KWh). While a medium-sized PV panel might provide an average of 50 watts, a larger panel can bring you above 200 watts.

A variety of solar calculators can be found online, including at the following websites:

www.findsolar.com
www.pvwatts.org
http://solar.sharpusa.com
www.thesolarguide.com

23

RUDOLPH'S NOT SO BRIGHT ANYMORE

No, Santa hasn't gone solar . . . yet. But come Christmastime, you can decorate the exterior of your home the eco-friendly way with strings of solar-powered lights. Sounds simple, but you will want to take the following into consideration before purchasing:

Different products will have differing illumination times. The average illumination period is about 7–8 hours, but daytime weather will ultimately determine how charged your lights are at night, and subsequently how long they stay lit.

The next question: blinking or steady? Some versions offer the best of both worlds via a switch that easily changes the twinkle factor.

Review the lights' battery requirements. Yes, solar-powered lights need a way to store charge—and that's where the battery comes in. Some manufacturers use non-rechargeable lithium batteries in their lights, while others use rechargeable batteries.

You can decorate the exterior of your home the eco-friendly way with strings of solar-powered lights.

Prepare for potential sticker shock: solar holiday lights will likely cost more than their traditional peers, but you'll notice the savings on your post-season utility bills.

Where to find them? If you're Internet savvy, try Googling "solar Christmas lights" and you'll find many vendors. Otherwise, inquire at your local stores for availability.

24
FIND A MAN TO DO YOUR BIDDING

If you're not confident or skilled enough to install your solar power system yourself, it's time to find a PV provider to do the work for you.

This will be an important relationship! Now that you have decided to take the plunge and invest your hard-earned money on renewable energy for your home, you want the process of researching options and installing your chosen system to be as smooth as possible. Finding the right PV provider for you could take some time; be patient and willing to wait until you've struck the right chord, both professionally and personally. Pay attention to your gut feelings—they won't steer you down the wrong path. Your stomach aside, here are some tips to keep in mind:

One of the best ways to find a quality installer is through referrals. Don't be shy about finding out as much as you can about your candidates—you'll save yourself from migraines later on in the process.

This is key: DOES THE INSTALLER HAVE THE TIME TO COMPLETE YOUR PROJECT IN A TIMELY MANNER? Why, you might be asking yourself right now, did I put that last sentence in cautionary CAPS? Because, I tell ya, human nature can be an unbridled Pollyanna. Make sure your interviews with candidates include a discussion about realistic timing. Also, keep yourself in check with your own expectations—are you in a hurry, do you want your solar system installed yesterday? Take a breath,

One of the best ways to find a quality installer is through referrals. Don't be shy about finding out as much as you can about your candidates— you'll save yourself from migraines later on in the process.

shake down those shoulders, and remember that this is a long-term investment of time and money. Be willing to compromise on the timing, but be ultra-careful when confronted with an installer who promises you the moon.

Ask to see your candidate's license, and take note of his license number. What renewable energy certification and/or training does he have under his belt? Does he understand local and national rebate scenarios that might save you money? Also, make sure the candidate has a valid contractor license and ask if he would be willing to post a performance bond (a guarantee that the job will be completed as per the contract) and whether he has an active worker's comp policy. Request an example of the bid process, and insist on clarity when it comes to how the candidate hires subcontractors and how he approaches and works with lenders.

Finally, if you have an attorney, it's wise to ask him to review all contracts before you embark on your solar adventure.

25

SHINING EXAMPLE

As president of Solar Design Associates (SDA), Steven Strong is at the forefront of solar technology and the integration of renewable energy systems. Named an environmental hero by *Time* magazine in 1999 and "Environmental Entrepreneur of the Year" by the Audubon Society in 2003—just two of many prestigious honors and awards—Strong has worked long and hard to advance the cause of moving away from fossil fuels and into a new realm of Earth-friendly energy.

Strong, who founded SDA in 1974, had been working prior to that as an engineering consultant on the Alaskan pipeline. That job convinced him there were "easier, less-costly and more environmentally desirable" ways to deal with the nation's energy needs than "going to the ends of the earth to extract the last drop of fossil fuel."

With his background in architecture and engineering, Strong has earned SDA an international reputation for finding new ways to integrate solar electricity into environmentally responsible design. His list of projects is too long for this book, but here are some highlights:

* Electric Sunflowers: SDA's response to clients who wanted to power their country home and vineyard in the Napa Valley. The clients mandated that the system be efficient, reliable, enjoyable to look at, and fun. Strong's company proposed a large array of electric sunflowers on a steep, south-facing hillside on the client's property. The sunflowers track the sun from dawn to dusk and then return to their starting place to begin the process again the next day. "Tracking enhances the solar harvest while creating what the clients refer to as a 'hillside of kinetic art,'" explains Strong. To see a photo of these magnificent sunflowers, go to **www.solardesign.com** and search under "Projects."

* Solar-Powered Gas Stations: When BP made the environmentally forward decision to use solar to power their gas stations, they hired SDA to design, engineer, and construct the appropriate solar array technology. Existing flat-panel canopies were topped with low-profile crystalline arrays. For new stations, SDA designed a shallow, barrel-vaulted canopy glazed with transparent PV elements.

* Solar-Powered Olympics: Strong's company provided design and engineering support to architects working on the Olympic Village for the 1996 summer games in Atlanta, Georgia. The Olympic Natatorium's main roof features a large PV array and a solar-thermal system to warm the competition pools. SDA also designed the custom arched-glass PV canopy that served as the entry to the Olympic venue.

GO SOLAR!

In August 2008, the U.S. Department of Energy (DOE) announced it would invest up to $24 million in fiscal year 2008 and beyond to develop solar energy products to "significantly accelerate penetration of solar photovoltaic (PV) systems in the United States."

The program aims to make electricity generated by PV systems cost-competitive with conventional grid-tied electricity by 2015. The Solar America Initiative (SAI) has partnered with industry, statewide universities, state governments, federal agencies, and other non-governmental agencies to boost the economy by creating a U.S.-based solar industry, as well as diversifying the nation's electricity portfolio, working to reduce the effects of power outages in major metropolitan areas, and reducing the overall environmental impact of power generation from fossil fuels, nuclear energy, and natural gas.

Also part of the initiative is the Solar America Cities program, which has gathered twenty-five U.S. cities to partner with the DOE to support the goals of SAI. Participating cities have expressed their commitment to accelerating the adoption and integration of solar technology at the local level. The cities are:

Seattle, WA	Milwaukee, WI
Portland, OR	Ann Arbor, MI
Berkeley, CA	Pittsburgh, PA
San Francisco, CA	Philadelphia, PA
Santa Rosa, CA	New York, NY
Sacramento, CA	Boston, MA
San Jose, CA	Austin, TX
San Diego, CA	Houston, TX
Salt Lake City, UT	San Antonio, TX
Denver, CO	New Orleans, LA
Tucson, AZ	Knoxville, TN
Minneapolis/St. Paul, MN	Orlando, FL
Madison, WI	

For more information, go to **http://www1.eere.energy.gov** and select the "Solar Energy Technologies" link.

27 WE CAN ECOBUILD AMERICA

Described as an event for architects, contractors, facility managers, planners, developers, engineers, government officials, homebuilders, building and construction product manufacturers, and anyone else interested in the fascinating juncture where "ecology meets technology," the annual Ecobuild America conference is one-stop shopping for those interested in emerging sustainable technologies and trends in the renewable energy sector as they pertain to building development and construction. The event offers a variety of workshops, seminars, and lectures on all things green. For more information, go to **www.EcobuildAmerica.com.**

FACE IT

- If you're planning to build a new home, take full advantage of passive solar by orienting the length of the building along an east-west axis. Place large windows on the south or southeast wall for maximum solar gain, and limit windows on the north- and west-facing walls.

28 LIGHT ON THE WALLET

Making the commitment to install a solar system in your home is not just a commitment to renewable energy, it's also a financial commitment with long-term benefits, including the fact that a PV array will increase the value of any home by approximately half the cost of the system in place.

Nonetheless, if money is tight and you still want to make the switch to solar, your timing in looking for a loan should be good and, with time, will get better. If you live in California, you are already ahead of the game, and if you happen to be a resident of Berkeley, you are among the very lucky: in September 2008, the Berkeley City Council unanimously approved an innovative new program that provides city-backed loans to homeowners for the purpose of installing PV systems. The loans, which average $22,000, are payable over 20 years and are attached to homeowners' property tax bills. Other cities have taken note of Berkeley's plan; while Berkeley's program is funded by bonds, Palm Desert, for example, is paying for a similar program with monies from its general fund.

And that's not all, California residents: the Helio Green Energy Plan is a creative alternative to financing residential solar installations. The plan allows homeowners to enjoy the benefits of solar power without having to front the costs. Each applicant is reviewed in order to determine energy needs. Helios then designs a system and installs it—no money is exchanged. The homeowner pays for the power provided by the PV panels and Helios provides free maintenance, though homeowners are required to cover any damage to the system via personal insurance. Six years after installation, the homeowner may purchase the system from Helio. Average cost? About $18,000. Kudos, California!

AND MONEY BACK

- Rebates for installing solar power systems are increasingly common, and they act as incentives to encourage consumers to build or retrofit with solar. Call your local utility to find out if you are eligible to receive a kickback on your purchase.

LET THE SUN SHINE IN

Here's a clever way to bring more natural light into your home: the Sun Tunnel, a tubular skylight that can be installed onto most rooftops. With a watertight circular design (which eliminates water buildup) and a leak-proof coated steel flashing that fits most roof styles, the Sun Tunnel arrives as a kit complete with detailed installation instructions. Why not just purchase a regular skylight and call it a day, you might be wondering? Here's what makes the Sun Tunnel special: its flexible tubing can be maneuvered to avoid structural obstructions in just about any roof, and the tubing consists of Sola-film, a highly reflective and long-lasting material. For more information, go to **www.bigfrogmountain.com.**

IT'S GETTING HOT IN HERE

If you've ever spent time in an attic, you know that they can get pretty . . . steamy. Attics trap the hot air that rises from the lower floors of a building, and if that air isn't released, the result is a hot, stuffy, for the most part inhospitable space.

That said, attic venting is important—it cools and extends the life span of the roof and roofing materials and reduces the

Now you can release all that hot air with a solar-powered attic fan installed on your roof.

load on air-conditioning systems. Venting all that stagnant air increases the circulation of fresh air through space, reducing vapor buildup generated by showering and cooking (excess moisture in an attic can lead to all kinds of problems, from rust and rot to bacteria growth and dangerous mold counts). Now, you can release all that hot air with a solar-powered attic fan installed on your roof. Called the Natural Light Solar Attic Fan, the device reduces the temperature of the attic, in turn reducing the effort put out by air-conditioning or another cooling system. The device has a venting capacity of up to 1,200 square feet and has an optional thermostat that automatically turns off the unit in colder weather. Ask your power company if your purchase of a solar attic fan qualifies for a rebate. For more information, go to **www.solaratticfans.com.**

31 SOLAR BEAUTIFUL

Add some beauty to a window with a solar-powered glass radiometer. The first radiometer was invented by English physicist Edward Crookes in 1870. He wanted to demonstrate, via a simple physics experiment, how light can be transformed into energy through movement. The result is a basic but functional solar power plant! It works like this: when exposed to light, the four vanes (shiny on one side and black on the other) balanced on a spindle in a partial vacuum begin to revolve. The black vane heats up faster than the shiny side, repelling air molecules from its warm surface. This tiny difference in air pressure causes the vanes to rotate. The brighter the light, the faster the rotation.

Solar radiometers are available from numerous online vendors. Simply do a search for "solar radiometer" and you'll get to a source.

GET A SOLAR MAKEOVER

* The American Solar Energy Society (ASES) is an excellent resource for all things solar. Call (303) 443-3130 or go to **www.ases.org** for more information.

FIELD OF GREEN

Baseball. It's a true-blue American tradition. Earnest fans. Hot dogs. Solar panels. Errr . . . solar panels? Yes, it's true. Professional baseball is officially on the green bandwagon thanks to the efforts of high-profile teams across the country. Read on.

The Boston Red Sox and the National Resources Defense Council have joined forces to turn Fenway Park into a green oasis. So far, Fenway has been equipped with 28 rooftop solar hot water heating panels that will reduce the natural gas currently used by about 30 percent. The park is also looking at solar-powered trash compactors and is beefing up its recycling program and bringing organic produce to concession stands.

At Coors Field, the Colorado Rockies' LED scoreboard runs on a 46-panel solar array that generates 9.9kW of power. The Rockies purchased the array through Xcel Energy.

The San Francisco Giants, who play at AT&T Park, are treating their fans the right way: organic hot dogs and microbrew are now available in concessions. The ballpark also boasts the largest PV array in Major League Baseball. Designed by Steven Strong's

Massachusetts-based Solar Design Associates (to learn more about solar pioneer Steven Strong, see page 49) and installed by PG&E, the system is composed of 590 solar cells capable of generating enough energy to power the team's new energy-efficient scoreboard.

The San Francisco Giants installed 590 solar panels on the exterior of their stadium to power a new scoreboard.

The Cleveland Indians, which call Jacobs Field home, were the first American League team to undergo a solar retrofit at their park. The team collaborated with Green Energy Ohio to install forty-two solar panels on a pavilion building.

33

SO COOL IT'S HOT

Solar-Cool Technologies has rolled out its solar-powered cooler. If you are thinking this is just another product, then you may have to think again. The reason being, this cooler saves time, money, and the environment. The cooler works like a utilitarian multipurpose charging tool for your laptops, phones, etc. (handy when you are out camping, picnicking, or just outdoors). More exciting than the solar concept is the cooler's capacity to keep things cool or hot (depending on what role you want it to play). With the sun's mercy, it can stay at 30 degrees below or 30 degrees above the present temperature. Isn't this cool? With respect to the environment, the makers claim that each cooler being used offsets 5,000 pounds of CO_2 per annum. The cost of this utility device is $250.

COOKIN' WITH SOLAR

Ready to become a solar-powered chef? Check out *Cooking with the Sun*, by Beth Halacy and Dan Halacy. This ingenious book offers everything from instructions for building a solar oven to a recipe for Solar Stew.

34

DON'T USE ALL YOUR ENERGY

Let's take a minute to review some proven ways of conserving energy. Every little step is a step in the right direction. How about:

* Using compact fluorescent light bulbs.
* Turning off the lights when you leave a room.
* Purchasing Energy Star appliances when possible (they use approximately 50 percent less energy than standard, older appliances).
* Installing water-saving showerheads.
* Turning furnaces down and air-conditioning controls higher.
* Finally repairing those drip-drip-dripping taps.
* Not leaving the refrigerator door open longer than absolutely necessary.
* Learning how to "hyper-mile"—a driving technique that saves fuel and has a calming effect!
* Cooking in a microwave instead of an oven—it's faster and, thus, more energy efficient.
* Buying a front-loading washing machine, which uses less water and energy than a standard top-loader.
* Planting native grasses and plants to reduce water consumption.
* Shopping in second-hand stores, looking for used goods online (eBay, etc.).
* Refusing to use disposable drinking cups, plates, and utensils.

* Reading the excellent *It's Easy Being Green*, by Crissy Trask, for many more ideas.

35
A FOREST OF SHADED PARKING

Parking lots—are they known for their aesthetic appeal? Not likely. More frequently they are quickly forgotten in-between points, segues to where you need to be. Robert Noble, the CEO of Envision Solar in La Jolla, California, wants to transform how we view parking lots by turning them into showcases of solar technology. His solar "trees" are designed to accommodate two plug-in hybrid cars. The trees provide a 120-volt socket for the cars so that they do not have to depend solely on their engines to recharge.

The design of the trees is straightforward but absolutely visionary: a single trunk supports a canopy inlaid with electricity-producing PV panels. Noble, having invested a lot of time thinking about the endless acres of unshaded (read: Hot! Unpleasant! Let's get out of here now!) paved parking lots stamped out across the United States, sees opportunity in what most of us see as a necessary but ugly blot on the landscape. The opportunity? For one, shade. Imagine it! Shaded parking lots. Consider the impact of this in a place like Phoenix, in the summer, and you get the significance. And how to shade? With groves of solar trees. Noble wants to "plant" groves of solar trees in parking lots to help shade all that asphalt. The solar panels on the trees' canopies would provide electricity for the parking lot.

And, should electric cars become more common and, thus, more in need of a place to sit and recharge, the symbiotic undercurrent of Noble's idea is clear. Beyond cars, Noble wants to plant his trees at public transit hubs and install solar groves for light-rail.

"Just as a citrus grove absorbs sunlight to produce food, a Solar Grove absorbs sunlight and produces energy."

According to the company, the Envision Solar Grove can be customized to meet individualized needs for a photovoltaic-integrated parking lot solar system. The Solar Grove, the company explains, "lends itself to a variety of surroundings and terrain that could otherwise prove challenging to more standard designs."

The design of the groves is based on the concept of "bio-mimicry," Envision says, adding, "Just as a citrus grove absorbs sunlight to produce food, a Solar Grove absorbs sunlight and produces energy. The language of the analogy continues—the frame and modules of the Solar Tree become its 'canopy,' the support structure becomes the 'limbs' and 'trunk,' while the base foundation and wiring beneath the earth is known as the 'taproot.'"

Beautifully said, Envision. We're rooting for you! (Pun sort of intended.) For more information, go to **www.envisionsolar.com.**

36

HUG THOSE TREES

The Internet is a vast, seemingly unlimited source of pretty much any kind of information you could ever want. But there's a catch: How much of that information can you trust to be accurate? And how many sites truly deserve their place in the giant web-o-sphere?

Enter a site that, without question, has earned its place as one of the best on the Web for all things green: **Treehugger.com.** The creation of ceramicist Graham Hill, Treehugger consistently makes the 25 Most Popular blogs list. Given that some 100,000 blogs are born each day around the world, that's a laudable accomplishment. That Treehugger has reached this level of success in the relatively short time since its debut in 2004 speaks to the quality of its content. The site has more than 60 writers who post some 50 articles per day, and it averages about 3 million visitors each month. How to describe it? Well, you really need to visit to capture its true brilliance, but suffice it to say that Treehugger is a clearinghouse of sorts—for articles about the environment and renewable technologies and information about books, films, and any number of deep-thought possibilities. Its latest coup: partnering with the cable network Planet Green. In the roiling sea of "www" that has become the Internet, Treehugger stands out. A word of caution: it's hard to read just one post, so give yourself some time to hang out and meander.

37

THE SKINNY ON YOUR SKIN

It seems everywhere we turn we are subjected to cautionary, sometimes terrifying, stories of the effects of exposing our unprotected skin to the rays of the sun. If we were to whole-heartedly side with the anti-sun Cassandras, we would indeed come to believe that those far-away rays do nothing beneficial to our bodies, but rather wreak havoc via wrinkled, leathery skin and deadly cancer. Absolutely, we must protect ourselves from too much sun exposure. Sunscreen works, and it should be used with a vigilance akin to choosing the right wine with dinner.

Our bodies need the healing rays of the sun in order to keep us topped off with adequate levels of vitamin D.

However, emerging medical research suggests that our bodies need the healing rays of the sun in order to keep us topped off with adequate levels of vitamin D, a nutrient vital to bone health and proper immune system function. Some doctors advocate scheduling up to 15 minutes per day of lotion-free sun exposure to keep D where it needs to be. As with all things, everything in moderation. Add a little sun to your days and the remainder of the time, use a good sunscreen. For more informa-tion on this topic, I suggest you visit **www.mercola.com.**

38

A GODLY ALLIANCE

Named in honor of the visionary Apollo space program, the Apollo Alliance is a coalition of business, labor, environmental, and community leaders that actively promotes clean energy technology and policy across the United States in the hope of reducing dependence on foreign oil, cutting environmentally damaging carbon emissions, and expanding "green sector" job opportunities. The group aims to create new jobs by promoting renewable energy policy and technology and strives to "put millions of Americans to work in a new generation of well-paid green collar jobs, and make America a global leader in clean energy products and services."

Founded in 2004, the Alliance believes the wisest route to job growth in the U.S. is via the green highway and that by extending convincing arguments for investing in clean energy technology, leaders in all sectors of business and government will respond favorably to an innovative approach to economic growth: one based on the concepts of clean energy. The group's New Energy for America report—an economic analysis of its Ten-Point Plan, which documents how the tax credits and investments it proposes would create more than 3 million new high-wage jobs in manufacturing, construction, transportation, high-tech and the public sector—is available for review at no cost at **www.apolloalliance.org.**

SUNNY STATES

Home Power magazine (required reading if you are serious about solar) has compiled a list of the 10 best states for solar energy. How did they decide who made the list? "Strong incentives, forward-thinking regulatory policies, and aggressive renewable energy goals are a good start. But what really gets the *Home Power* crew excited is any state that takes serious steps from a fossil fuel–based economy to a solar-based one."

Some of the winners might surprise you. Drum roll, please...

California; average statewide daily peak sun-hours: 5.6
Colorado; sun-hours: 5.8
Connecticut; sun-hours: 4.4
Maryland; sun-hours: 4.6
Massachusetts; sun-hours: 4.6
Minnesota; sun-hours: 4.5
New Jersey; sun-hours: 4.6
New Mexico; sun-hours: 6.2
Oregon; sun-hours: 4.4
Pennsylvania; sun-hours: 4.3

40

BLOW THAT HOT AIR

Canadian solar engineering firm Solarwall has developed a heating and ventilation system that looks like traditional metal cladding but doubles as a heater. A Solarwall system costs about the same as construction of a metal wall but provides free heating and ventilation for the life of the building. The Solarwall is an unglazed solar collector that uses perforated sheet metal to preheat ventilation air. Savings depend on geographical location, but are generally in the range of $2 to $8 per square foot per year. For more information, visit **www.solarwall.com.**

POWER UP!

One of the most innovative solar products now on the market, Power Film has a variety of uses that place it firmly in the top spot of renewable energy technology. Just thirteen inches wide and up to 2,400 feet long, the rolled-up panels are constructed with a flexible yet durable polyamide substrate, which provides a paper-thin and lightweight panel as thin as 0.025 millimeters. The absorber layer is amorphous silicon, and the amount of silicon used is as low as 1 percent of the amount used in traditional panels.

The maker of Power Film has a long list of the material's potential applications; they include metal roofing, where it is conformable to a variety of architectural styles; membrane roofing, for use on commercial buildings, schools, hospitals, and warehouses; and architectural fabric, such as canopies, covered walkways, sports stadiums, airports, and convention centers. For more information, go to **www.powerfilmsolar.com.**

COOL SHADES FOR WINDOWS

For a relatively inexpensive way to cool the interiors of your home, reduce glare, and protect your furniture and carpeting from fading, consider covering your windows with sheets of window-tinting material. *Real Goods* offers affordable tinting kits for a variety of window sizes and claims its tinting film reduces UV transmission by 97 percent and decreases heat penetration inside the home by 60 percent. The material can be applied easily to wet windows or Plexiglas, and it is held in place by static electricity, not adhesive. What happens when the season shifts and you want to invite that warming heat into your home? It's simple: just peel off the material and let the sun shine in.

Other types of window tinting kits are available online. Just do a search for "window tint kit" and you should find plenty of options.

THIS ROOF'S ON FIRE

One of the most compelling advances in solar technology is the solar shingle, which looks like an ordinary roof shingle but is composed of thin-film PV cells. Despite their next-to-nothing profile, amorphous silicon shingles are powerful harnessers of the sun's energy. In addition, they tend to be more powerful than regular solar panels due to their ramped-up efficiency and ability to absorb more sunlight than other solar options on the market. Their thinness does not equate with flimsiness, either: the reality is that solar shingles are sturdy and long lasting and as such are a wise investment.

In most cases, solar shingles require an under-decking of ventilated plywood to mitigate the great quantities of heat they absorb. They also protect the house itself: when positioned in the same overlapping fashion as regular shingles, they protect the roof from the sun and other effects from the weather.

> # The silicon shingles are powerful harnessers of the sun's energy, and tend to be more powerful than regular solar panels due to their ability to absorb more sunlight than other solar options on the market.

The shingles' wiring is threaded through the roof deck and connected to the solar inverter. They are impervious to shifting thanks to the heavy-duty heat-activated glue used to attach them to the roof. Estimates reveal that the shingles pay for themselves over their average 20-year life span.

Besides providing solar power in an efficient, low-profile manner, the shingles can be the perfect solution in neighborhoods where regular PV panels might be met with resistance. Solar panel shingles blend easily with other roof materials, making them practically invisible from a distance.

GLOW-IN-THE-SUN PAINT

If research and development continues as planned, the latest product in the solar technology arsenal should be available soon. Inexpensive PV paint has been invented in the United Kingdom in a joint venture between researchers at Swansea University and the steel industry and is pushing its way toward production and commercial availability. Imagine the possibilities! The paint, composed of dye and electrolytes that can be applied as a paste to sheets of steel, has the potential to change how buildings integrate solar power systems into their inner workings. Four layers of paint are applied to each sheet of metal. When light hits the solar cells, the molecules within release electrons into an electron collector and circuit. Then, the electrons move back into the dye.

Solar paint has some advantages over PV panels. For one, it can absorb light across the visible spectrum, which means that production of solar-generated electricity would not stop or be hindered on cloudy days. And for that we wish the developers nothing but success!

45

RIDING TOWARD THE LIGHT

Now this is really something to smile about: a solar-powered motorized bicycle. The invention of an innovative and eco-minded man named Peter Sandler, the E-V Sunny "photo-optic" bike can be had for a cool $1,795. Developed in Canada, the E-V Sunny boasts PV panels that transform it from a run-of-the-mill two-wheeler to an altogether novel form of transportation.

This bike is not for racing, though: with its all-aluminum frame, sun-powered motor, and battery, it weighs in at about 44 pounds. The bike's front hub motor is fully encased and waterproof and rated to 350 watts. Speeds of up to 18 miles per hour are possible with the bike's power-assist feature.

For now the bikes are a special-order specialty item, but let's hope we see more of them on the road, and soon. Fortunately, the E-V Sunny has a top-quality saddle seat with "comfort sus-pension"—because even greenies like a little cush on the tush.

For more information go to **www.therapyproducts.com.**

46

MORE FLEXIBLE THAN A GYMNAST

The solar energy sector is aiming to make the technology as versatile and user-friendly as possible. To that end, rigid solar panels have morphed into flexible versions that are easy to use, lightweight, and transportable, making them ideal in a variety of situations, such as when a portable power system is needed. No longer relegated to a fixed-in-place existence, flexible solar panels can be folded or rolled up and easily stowed for hiking, camping, and travel.

Flexible solar panels are manufactured in a process called thin-film deposition, which applies thin layers of superconducting silicon onto a substrate that can be flexed, folded, and bent. Putting a flexible solar panel to work involves little more than unrolling it and placing it in a sunny location. The use options are abundant and include charging mobile phones and laptops, as well as marine and RV batteries.

LIGHT YEARS AHEAD: AL GORE

No book about the environment would be complete without a mention of Al Gore, the man who seems to have already lived many lifetimes in one. The former vice president appears to have moved seamlessly from the world of politics to assume the title of environmental guru.

A full list of Gore's accomplishments would take considerably more space than these pages can offer, but a summary is warranted. Let's start with his winning the 2007 Nobel Peace Prize, an event that provided him with a world stage on which to reiterate his years-long warning about global warming, that it is "the greatest challenge we've ever faced." He went on to say, "We face a true planetary emergency. The climate crisis is not a political issue, it is a moral and spiritual challenge to all of humanity."

> ## "The climate crisis is not a political issue, it is a moral and spiritual challenge to all of humanity."

When Gore's documentary film, *An Inconvenient Truth*, won two Oscars, it became evident without question that the world was paying attention to his words of caution and finding solace in his hopeful vision for fixing what is wrong.

A prolific writer, Gore has authored numerous articles and books, including *The Assault on Reason*, *An Inconvenient Truth* (in both book and DVD format), *Earth in the Balance*, and *Joined at the Heart*.

Gore continues to devote his time to a variety of projects, including The Alliance for Climate Protection, The Climate Project, Live Earth, An Inconvenient Truth, and Generation Investment Management. To learn more about this dynamic environmental leader, go to **www.algore.com.**

48
BAN THE HUMVEE— GET A SUNVEE!

If you want to wow the neighbors and make a statement about renewable energy, take a look at the SunVee.

SunVee stands for "solar utility neighborhood vehicle." It features solar panels integrated into the body, which charge batteries that in turn power an electric motor. Billed as a "practical vehicle for trips with passengers and cargo," the SunVee has a range of about 30 miles and a top speed of 25 miles per hour.

The SunVee concept is the work of Kelly Hart, who designed and built his first solar vehicle in 1999—the Sunmobile, powered both by solar energy and pedaling.

See for yourself: **www.sunvee.com.**

CUP OF SOLAR BREW

Did you know that:

* In the United States alone, some 400 million cups of coffee are consumed every day? No surprise, then, that the U.S. is the world's leading coffee consumer.
* Coffee accounts for 75 percent of all the caffeine consumed in the United States.
* Every year, more than 100 million bags of coffee make their way to market.

In a word, WOW. So we like our coffee. And, if you are reading this book, you are likely an eco-conscious consumer who looks for ways to support businesses that don't place profits over the health of the planet.

Enter brothers Dave and Mike Hartkop, purveyors of fine coffee. Why are they different from any other coffee roaster? Because they roast their beans using the power of the sun.

Dave and Mike are the founders of Solar Roast Coffee (**www.solarroast.com**), which began in Oregon and now operates out of sunny Pueblo, Colorado. They roast their coffee in a marvelous device of their own invention: the Helios 4 solar concentrator, an upgraded and more powerful model of the original roaster that can roast 30 pounds of coffee in as little as 15–25 minutes. The roaster features a large mirror array situated on a motorized rotating platform, which allows the unit to follow the sun across its arc in the sky, from its rising in the east to its setting in the west. That's not all this sophisticated roaster can do: it is also equipped with a winch system that can tip the entire array up (like a large easel, the brothers explain) to follow the path of the sun vertically as it rises and sets. Solar panels power the motors. On cloudy days, a conventionally powered back-up heat source allows business to proceed uninterrupted. The Helios 4 is a far cry from the brothers' initial design: an old satellite dish covered with plastic mirrors.

Solar Roast Coffee offers retail and wholesale purchasing options. For ordering information, call (719) 544-3515 or browse the Hartkop's entertaining website, where you can also order a compostable traveler's coffee mug made from plastic derived from corn plants.

SEARCHING FOR
BRIGHT IDEAS

Located in Golden, Colorado, and Washington, D.C., the National Renewable Energy Laboratory (NREL) is the primary research center and lab for renewable energy and energy-efficient research and development in the United States. The lab began operating in 1977 as the Solar Energy Research Institute. In 1991 it was desig-nated a national laboratory of the U.S. Department of Energy (DOE) and its name was changed to NREL. The lab aims to advance the energy goals of the DOE's Office of Energy Efficiency and Renew-able Energy and beyond, guiding renewable energy goals from research and development to the commercial marketplace.

Solar technology is a key area of R&D at the lab. Its Solar

Energy Technologies Program performs research in two major areas of renewables: photovoltaics and solar thermal. The lab's PV work involves research into PV-related materials, the development of PV cells in several material systems, and working with the PV industry to speed up the manufacturing capacity and market availability of PV technologies.

Regarding solar thermal, the lab is working with the solar industry to lower the cost of solar water-heating systems through the creation and testing of new polymer materials and is developing parabolic trough technology (a reliable power source for large-scale utility plants) for solar electricity generation. Although trough technology is not yet financially feasible in today's energy market, the lab aims to reduce costs associated with the technology so that it can become a viable component of the nation's energy equation.

A visitor center is located at the Golden site and can be reached at (303) 384-6565. For information on job opportunities, call the public affairs office at (303) 275-4090. And, to learn more about the lab's many areas of research and development, go to **www.nrel.gov.**

POOL POWER

If you own a swimming pool, you already know it takes plenty of cash to keep the water clean and warm. Reduce your eco-footprint by replacing your grid-connected heating and cleaning system with a solar-powered alternative. AAA Solar of New Mexico has a system that will keep your pool fresh and comfortable for about $1,075–$2,490, fully installed.

52

BY THE LIGHT OF THE {SOLAR-POWERED} LANTERN

The lovely Isabella catalog (**www.IsabellaCatalog.com**) features beautiful Chinese-inspired lanterns that can be strung up in trees and around patios—and which are powered by the sun. This means no wires or plugs to contend with (and disrupt the eye-soothing scene). When placed for maximum sun exposure, the lanterns soak up sunshine and, when the light fades, automatically light up.

Constructed of weather-resistant, silk-like nylon, the lanterns are available (as of this writing) in square and teardrop shapes and are a very reasonable price of $24.95. When fully charged with the included AAA rechargeable battery, they provide 6–8 hours of dreamy, ethereal light. Whoever created these must be a nice person.

LIGHT UP THE RADIO

Gama Sonic's portable solar lamp with built-in AM/FM radio solves two issues at once: the need for light and the need for music and news. The lamp is useful in the outdoors (camping, sailing, anywhere an outlet is not available) and features an upper torch for reading. It comes with an AC/DC adapter that will charge the rechargeable battery at home at night, and its solar panel can be adjusted for maximum sun exposure.

Gama Sonic also manufactures solar-charged lights for sheds, garages, greenhouses, and boat houses; solar accent lights and spotlights for eco-friendly landscaping; an ingenious solar-powered address light that makes it possible to see the street number in the dark (the device charges by day and automatically turns on at night); a solar-powered flashlight with key chain that charges in just 30 minutes; and a patio umbrella constructed with LED lights embedded into its inner upper poles. The umbrella's solar panel sits discreetly atop the canopy, omitting the need for extra wiring. It uses a rechargeable battery to hold the day's solar reserves. For more information go to **www.gamasonic.com.**

54

SUN-POWERED PRIUS

The Toyota Prius, the hybrid vehicle that has become a symbol of environmental enlightenment and is the most fuel-efficient car sold in the United States, just got even better. The redesigned third-generation 2010 Prius has an average fuel economy of 50 mpg and can reach 60 miles per hour faster than earlier models. But it's the latest feature—a tilt-and-slide moonroof embedded with solar panels capable of generating enough power to run the air conditioner on hot days—that has enviro-types wagging their tongues all the way to car dealers nationwide.

With its decision to give consumers the option of the Kyocera solar cells on its high-end version of the car, now the world's most popular hybrid, Toyota became the first major automaker to integrate solar technology into a vehicle.

Says the company: "When the vehicle is parked in direct sunlight, these solar panels power a fan that brings in outside air, ventilating the cabin close to ambient temperature. The cool technology continues with a button on the key fob that activates that air conditioning system within 30 yards of the vehicle. The cabin will cool to the pre-set temperature level, without turning on the engine."

For more information on the 2010 Prius, go to **www.toyota.com.**

55

SOLAR INNOVATOR: ANSON FOGEL

Who: *Owner and CEO of Carbondale, Colorado–based Inpower Systems, which provides retail solar power setups and green energy consulting.*

TMO: Do most people know what they want when they walk through your doors?
FOGEL: Usually not, so we are careful to go through all the necessary steps to educate them and also determine what they truly need to reduce their fuel and electricity consumption. We discuss economics. If someone is looking to make a new house solar [versus a retrofit], we work on how to make that building as energy efficient as possible from the start.

TMO: What is one of the biggest concerns clients express regarding solar?
FOGEL: Aesthetics. It has to look good. Americans tend to buy with their hearts and egos, so if you can make it fun and cool and visually pleasing, then people can relate to it on an emotional level, and they'll invest in it.

TMO: Tell us about the PowerView software you developed. What does it do?

FOGEL: It tracks, in real time, how much energy a client's house is using or creating at any given moment. Clients love to be that closely connected to their energy habits. (For more information on PowerView, see #56, page 90.)

56

SUNNY TV

One of the greatest joys of investing in solar energy goes beyond the thrill of knowing that you are doing your bit for the planet. It comes when you can actually see how your investment is paying off, day by day, hour by hour.

Purveyors of PV panels understand the enormity of that thrill, and as such increasing numbers of them are working to offer their customers the ability to watch their PV cells in action.

Customers can log on to an individual account and watch their solar systems operate in real time.

One such company is Colorado-based InPower Systems (see #55, page 89), which has developed its own monitoring software called PowerView. PowerView makes it possible for customers to log on to an individual account and watch their solar systems operate in real time; they can track carbon saved, energy produced, and energy bought and sold.

PowerView, says company founder Anson Fogel, also serves as the clients' automatic connection to InPower Systems' service department. In other words, let's say your PVs don't seem to be operating at full potential. Maybe they're a little down in the dumps, you reason. PowerView takes the mystery out of the equation, says Fogel, adding, "If your solar system has any problem at any time, we'll dispatch a service technician to fix it within 48 hours—we're usually aware of any issues before you are."

PowerView is included in the price of some of the solar packages InPower sells, and upgrades can be purchased if desired. Check out the live demo at **www.inpowersystems.com.**

A SUNSHINY DAY OF EVENTS

Solar Power International: **www.solarpowerconference.com**

Ecobuild America: Sustainable, Green and High-Performance Solutions for the Built Environment: **www.EcobuildAmerica.com**

Green Business Conference: **www.coopamerica.biz**

Greenbuild International Conference & Expo: **www.greenbuildexpo.org**

WORD TO THE WISE

* This you need to know: some state rebate programs actually penalize consumers who install their own solar energy systems rather than hire a licensed contractor to do the work. Make sure you know the exact requirements of your state's rebate/incentive program before you begin.

NOW FOR A LITTLE LIGHT POETRY

Learning to Praise Again

With brusque scent of warmed sagebrush
the longtime sun reappears in the field
and renders the tall graying grass into gold.

Exhausted, I sought what was missing.
Instead, I find what was here all along:
the rising, the rising again, the rising again

and the myth of the rising, the faithful sun
at the center. Tale of night. Unfaithful worship.
Fable of cloud and day.

Under foot, crumbling, waning, change.
Prickly pear spines where pink coral grew.
Mesas fallen and falling. Last wing. Lost map.

And the sunlight braids its long fingers
through the wind's mutinous mane

and strokes a glaze to what is here,

doesn't care if we chant or repent or pray.
Even now, even now, even now it shines
whether we're worthy or not.

—*Rosemerry Wahtola Trommer*

Organic fruit grower and life-lover Rosemerry Wahtola Trommer lives near Telluride, Colorado, where she serves as poet laureate of San Miguel County. Visit her at www.wordwoman.com.

59 INVALUABLE WEBSITES

The following websites will keep you up-to-date on advances in solar technology and policy:

www.popularlogistics.com
www.huffingtonpost.com

www.metaefficient.com
www.solarbuzz.com

60 A CITY THAT'S LIGHT YEARS AHEAD

Meet the eco-city of Freiburg, a twelfth-century town located in the southwestern part of Germany. Freiburg has a population of just 217,000, but it has become famous the world over for its dedication to renewable energy sources, particularly solar. The town has become an eco-tourist destination, thanks to such marvels as the Heliotrope, a rotating house equipped with a large rooftop solar panel that tracks the sun, absorbing its energy. Designed by solar architect Rolf Disch, Heliotrope is just one example of how Freiburg has embraced solar technology. Solar panels are seemingly everywhere in this sunny hamlet, including on the town's soccer stadium and incorporated into entire neighborhoods.

The Freiburg city council thrust the municipality into the renewable energy sector back in 1992, with a broad-sweeping resolution that revealed a strong commitment to renewable alternatives. For example, the council mandated that all new structures on city land be "low-energy"—in other words, that they focus on both active and passive solar energy.

More than a third of Freiburg's residents do not drive a car and, according to a special National Geographic report on climate change, per capital carbon dioxide emissions in the area have fallen 10 percent in the last decade.

Nonetheless, the town still has far to go: despite its heroic attempts to transition into renewable energy, less than 1 percent of its electricity comes from the sun.

PLANTING A NEW WAVE OF SOLAR

The country of Dubai is often in the news for its spectacular architectural development. Now, the country with no lack of sunshine is poised to enter into solar manufacturing technology with the construction of the world's largest solar panel production plant.

The Solar Technologies FZE photovoltaic production facility is expected to come online in late 2010 and will produce PV panels capable of generating 130 megawatts of power on an annual basis.

The announcement of the plant was made at the Green Dubai World Forum 2008. Plans are for a 1 million-square-foot plant at Dubai's Technopark.

62

POWER IN THE BAG

Solar power has entered the realm of haute couture. Check out the clever handbag designed by C'N'C Costume National. For a cool $1,905, you can acquire the leather and suede satchel-style tote, which features a small built-in PV panel that allows the lady on the go to charge her cell phone and iPod without having to search for an electrical outlet. As of this writing, the bag was available at Tru Grace, (914) 273-9600. Though not couture, Noon Solar's functional and subtly stylish Sawyer messenger bag is equipped with a solar panel designed to charge its lithium-ion battery, but its eco-stature doesn't stop there. The bag is made from leather and dyed hemp, and is 100 percent biodegradable. The company also offers a nice variety of other savvy designs. The Sawyer bag retails for $375. For more information about the company and its vision, go to www.noonsolar.com.

COOKING LIGHT

Don't be intimated by the thought of cooking with solar. It can be a great (and zero-cost) alternative to conventional methods. All solar cookers work in a similar way: they focus the rays of the sun into a concise area and retain the heat gain, capable of reaching up to 600 degrees. You don't have to spend a fortune to get one, either: how does $40 sound? And it can fold to a portable 13-inch square, so you can take it on your next camping trip. Of course you could spend more, but aside from aesthetics and price, any properly built solar oven can roast meats, fish, and chicken; bake cookies, cakes, and breads (yum: muffins!); steam vegetables; and boil pasta, lentils, beans, and rice to perfection.

Using the sun to cook food and pasteurize water (thus preventing waterborne diseases) has been a lifesaver in developing countries, and humanitarian organizations are working hard to provide basic solar ovens to communities across the globe, in the process vastly improving quality of life and helping to slow the devastating effects of deforestation and desertification caused by burning wood.

Here's a quick run-down of how solar ovens work their magic:

1. **Concentrating sunlight**: A mirror or reflective metal concentrates the sun's rays into a small, well-defined cooking area. One solar cooker even uses an accordion-fold reflective car sunshade to trap that potent energy. Talk about multi-tasking!

2. **Turning light into heat**: The color black is key here, as it makes the cooker work more efficiently. For example, a black pan will absorb sunlight and convert it to heat. Also, the better a pan conducts heat, the faster the oven will work, but keep in mind that solar cooking is going to be a different experience than throwing a frozen dinner into the microwave. Cooking with the sun takes longer than conventional methods, but the trade-off is that it requires less hands-on time.

3. **Retaining heat**: The cooker won't work if precious captured heat is allowed to escape. You can trap heat with either a plastic bag or a glass cover. Trapping heat is especially important on chilly, overcast days, because it will help the cooker reach its desired temperature.

Most solar ovens tap into at least two of these techniques to produce the high temperatures required for cooking. A quick Web search will put you in touch with organizations that promote solar cooking and help you locate manufacturers of a wide range of ovens, from the rustic and basic to the more refined and elegant. You can even learn to build your own solar oven. Here are a few sites to get you started: **www.solarovens.org** and **www.solarcooking.org**. Kids (and adults, too, let's be fair) will enjoy the solar cooking lesson at **www.pbskids.org/zoom/activities/sci/solarcookers.html**.

SUNNY-SIDE UP!

Many of us tried this as kids, but we could never quite get it right, ending up with a mess of uncooked or partially cooked eggs all over the road. If you want to prove your cooking-eggs-on-pavement prowess, try this method for perfect eggs. Pass the salt!

The following technique is courtesy of Gavin D.J. Harper and is featured in his wonderful book, *Solar Energy Projects for the Evil Genius: 50 Do-It-Yourself Projects*.

First you will need eggs, oil, and a hot, sunny day. Add to that a black cast-iron frying pan, a sheet of glass, and an asphalt surface.

If eggs aren't your thing, try baking a batch of cookies using the dashboard of your car!

Place the pan on the asphalt, add the oil, and cover the pan with the glass. Both the pan and the asphalt will soak up the sun's heat, and this heat will transfer to the cooking oil. Crack an egg into the pan and watch as it begins to cook immediately. Again cover the pan with the glass. The result? An evenly cooked breakfast, sunny-side up.

If eggs aren't your thing, try baking a batch of cookies using the dashboard of your car! It has been done, successfully, even. And who needs an air freshener when your olfactory cells can be treated to the aroma of fresh chocolate chip confections? Here's how to do it: place drops of cookie dough on a black baking tray. (Remember to use a black tray; other colors will derail your culinary experiment, although eating cookie dough is not a shabby alternative.) Place the tray on the dashboard of your car, make sure all the windows are rolled up, and park in a sunny spot. A few hours later, voilà! Cookies for the drive home.

65
SUNNY NEWS, FOR REAL

The Internet is a sprawling, sometimes unwieldy, informational beast. You can click your way to just about any topic and opinion on said topic, but the problem is you can't always rely on the veracity of what you find. Let's take a moment to thank the very wonderful **www.solarbuzz.com** for vetting the following solar-themed daily news sites. Solar Buzz calls itself a "portal to the world of solar energy" and the description could not be more true. So, click away! You're in good hands.

Solar Industry News from National Renewable Energy
   Laboratories, National Center for Photovoltaics (USA/Global)
Solar News online from **WorldNews.com** (USA)
Green Building News by Iris Communications Inc. (USA)
News Stories about Solar: The Energie Letter, E-mail from IWR
   (in German/English) (Germany)
News Stories (and archives) of Sandia National Laboratories
   (USA)
Energy Publications News Service, Energy-Tech online (USA)
Solar Brief (in German, French, English) (Germany)
Green Energy News (USA)
Green Power Daily News from Green Power Network (USA)
Renewable Energy News from SolarAccess (USA)
Renewable Energy News from Caddet (the Centre for the Analysis
   and Dissemination of Demonstrated Energy Technologies)
   (USA)
Renewable Energy News (from **WorldsNews.com**) (USA)
Environmental News Service (from Lycos) (USA)

66 SOLAR CITY

Elon Musk, the co-founder of PayPal, has a strong interest in green technology. One of his latest ventures is SolarCity, a company committed to "providing sustainable, cost-effective solar solutions for many applications, from a single-family home to a commercial property."

SolarCity wants to make it possible for the mass market to obtain solar technology in an economically viable way. Its SolarLease program offers economic assistance to homeowners who want to switch to solar. Financing packages include low initial payments, which enable the consumer to benefit from solar without having to worry about high up-front costs, and a no-stress pay-as-you-go monthly lease payment plan.

SolarCity currently services the following areas:

San Francisco Bay Area, CA
San Jose, CA
Los Angeles, CA
Fresno, CA
San Diego, CA
Sacramento, CA
Portland, OR
Phoenix, AZ

For more information, go to **www.solarcity.com.**

STUDENTS OF THE SUN

Future generations of Earth's stewards are learning about solar technology thanks to the Pacific Gas and Electric Company's (PG&E) Solar Schools Program, which provides funding for grid-connected solar electricity installations designed to teach students about the benefits of renewable energy. The preferred system size is 1 kilowatt because it is both relatively inexpensive and can be installed quickly, and a small PV system can be placed for maximum visibility for students and the local neighborhood. Why the emphasis on visibility? The company explains: "This is because they [the solar panels] will remind each class of students that enters the school that part of their electricity is coming from solar energy. And because the systems will be up for years, each new generation will not know life without just a little bit of solar electricity, and we hope that that little bit goes a long way."

In addition to reducing schools' power bills by 1–2 percent, the systems are being integrated into curricula for science, math, history, and art. Each system is connected to an online data monitoring service that allows students and the community at large to observe real-time solar electricity production and witness firsthand the environmental impact of clean, renewable energy. Furthermore, students can compare the PV power of their school with other schools across the state. In northern and central California, teachers can sign up for free one-day solar energy training workshops.

Based in San Francisco, the Pacific Gas and Electric Company is one of the largest combination natural gas and electric utilities in the United States. In partnership with the Foundation for

Environmental Education, the company aims to donate a PV system to 40 K–12 public schools each year. Any K–12 public school within the PG&E service area that is currently getting its electricity from PG&E is eligible to apply, and schools within underserved or rural communities will receive first priority in the selection process.

For more information, go to **http://www.pge.com/solarschools/**.

68 LIGHTEN YOUR TAXES

The collective cheer that went up the day it was announced that federal financial incentives for solar installations had been extended was not just jubilant—it was a roar of happiness tinged with relief and fresh hope for the future of renewable energy.

Here's what happened: in late 2008, after Congress had tried for months to come to consensus on an extension of renewable energy tax credits, the House of Representatives swept in and passed the green incentive plan, attached to a broad-sweeping financial bailout package, and the president signed it into law, setting the stage for what some in the photovoltaics industry have dubbed the "solar boom."

Here are the highlights of the legislation:

* Extends the 30 percent solar investment tax credit to year 2016.
* Lifts the $2,000 tax credit limit for residential solar, which means that homeowners are eligible for a 30-percent tax credit on PV systems installed after Dec. 31, 2008.
* Utility companies are now eligible for a 30-percent investment tax credit for large-scale PV installations.

69
GOOGLE YOUR WAY TO SOLAR SAVVY

The founders of RoofRay do not consider themselves "green freaks," but, as they explain, they do believe in "good steward-ship of our planet." Realists at heart, they subscribe to the idea that "the economics [of a solar installation] must make sense for meaningful success."

RoofRay's goal is to help future consumers of solar technology ascertain whether a PV system is financially sensible by assisting them in evaluating solar for their home or business. Founded in 2008 as a response to high gas prices, RoofRay plans to offer a number of services, including:

* Showing the potential solar power user how a solar array could be set up on their roof.

* Explanation of the costs involved.

* Analysis of what others have done in their area.

* How to use their RoofRay "solar modeling" calculator, which allows users to drag and drop a tool to figure out slope, power potential, peak, and PV panel orientation.

The service uses Google Maps to locate the property in question. The user is also asked to enter an average monthly utility bill total, current electricity usage, and bills for an entire year to tally across-the-board savings.

For more information, go to **www.roofray.com.**

SHOW SOME DSIRE

No, we didn't accidentally leave out a letter in that header! DSIRE is short for Database of State Incentives for Renewable Energy. The DSIRE website, located at **www.dsireusa.org,** is a wealth of information on renewable energy incentives and regulatory policies administered by federal and state agencies and local organizations. Information is provided for each state, and the site's homepage features a U.S. map for quick access to individual states' policies and incentives. This is one-stop browsing if you want to find out if your state offers rebates for renewable energy installations and net metering, for example, and exactly which types of technologies are eligible (photovoltaics, wind energy, insulation, etc.). The site also offers a glossary of incentives; links to other renewable energy resources on the Web; a library of renewable energy policy reports, papers and presentations involving DSIRE; and new listings and updates to current policies. By tracking information on state, utility, local, and selected federal incentives that promote the use of renewable energy technologies, DSIRE is able to keep current on financial incentives for end-users who invest in renewables; those incentives include tax credits and deductions, grants, rebates, low-interest loans and bond programs. In addition, the site gives detailed information on the rules, regulations, and policies that affect the renewable technology sector.

71

GARDENING BRILLIANCE

If, like me, you yearn to grow a lush, abundant garden but live in a locale with a short growing season, help is on the way thanks to a brilliant book by New England "solar" gardeners Leandre Poisson and Gretchen Vogel Poisson titled *Solar Gardening*.

The advice and instructions inside are clear and concise if you've got a bit of the do-it-yourself in you and are comfortable following directions (or you know someone who is; I often summon my structural engineer husband for tasks like this). In summary, the book explains how to harness the growing power of direct sunlight even during the coldest months of the year and also how to protect young plants from becoming scorched during the summer, with the end result a gardener's dream: a year-round crop of organic veggies. Even small gardens, the authors claim, can yield a generous bounty across the calendar year. And all of this can be accomplished "off the grid" because properly focused sunshine replaces the need for energy derived from fossil fuels.

Whatever the season, the Poissons posit, plants will be equally happy in deadly heat and freezing cold when protected by Sun Pods and Sun Cones—simple but infinitely clever solar "appliances" designed by the authors. (The cones were inspired by the bell-shaped glass cloches that have been used by French gardeners since the days of Louis XIV.) The shape of the cones facilitates an atmosphere of optimal heat and moisture for seedlings and young plants and protects them from insects, hungry animals, and humidity-sapping wind.

LET IT ALL HANG OUT

Laundry, that everyday household chore we all love to avoid, consumes lots of energy. The good news is that washing machines that feature the U.S. Department of Energy's "Energy Guide" label, which provides specific information about how much energy, measured in kilowatt hours (kWh), the unit in question consumes, do indeed reduce energy consumption.

Wash your clothes in your environmentally friendly washing machine and then tap into limitless solar power by hanging them on an outside line to dry.

You've likely also seen appliances with an Energy Star rating. Energy Star, a joint program of the Environmental Protection Agency and the Department of Energy, notifies consumers of the most energy-efficient and eco-friendly appliances on the market. On average, according to the DOE, washing machines with the Energy Star designation use up to 50 percent less energy than their non-labeled peers.

So far so good, right? Well, not exactly. As washing machines have made significant advances in their energy efficiency prowess, clothes dryers have fallen behind the eco-wagon. The unfortunate reality is that, as of this writing, there is no require-ment that dryers display the Energy Guide label, which makes comparing the efficiency (or non-efficiency) of different models difficult. And, as the astute folks over at the *Real Goods Solar Living Source Book* point out, "Manufacturers [of clothes dryers] have little incentive to improve efficiency."

Harrumph! But there is a way around this discrepancy. Wash your clothes in your environmentally friendly washing machine and then tap into limitless solar power by hanging them on an outside line to dry. Alternately, you can hang them on a rack indoors, in a room with plenty of natural light.

If drying your clothes and linens outdoors is not an option and you don't have enough indoor space for the task, there are ways to increase the efficiency of your dryer. One of the most important things you can do is clean the lint filter after each use; allowing it to become clogged will reduce airflow in the machine and increase drying time (and can be a safety hazard, to boot). Also, wait until you have a full load to begin drying and, if you have more than one load to dry, dry each one back to back to soak up the machine's residual heat. Finally, check the outdoor exhaust vent: is it clear and clean? Make sure the flapper is not stuck or hindered from opening and closing.

73
SAN FRAN SOLAR

Nice job, San Francisco! In June 2008, Mayor Gavin Newsom signed into law an innovative new solar incentive program to encourage more PV installations. The city and county of San Francisco will now offer incentives to residents and businesses that install PV systems on their own properties. The program, called GoSolarSF, combined with federal tax credits and the California Solar Initiative, could pay for up to half the cost or more of a PV system installed within the city's boundaries. GoSolarSF provides incentives ranging from $3,000 to $6,000 for residents and up to $10,000 for businesses, and low-income residents can qualify for $5,000.

74 SUNNY MYTHS AND LEGENDS

Myth: Electricity generated by solar power cannot serve any significant portion of the electricity needs of the United States or the world.

Fact: PV technology can meet electricity demand at any scale. To illustrate: the solar energy potential in a 100-square-mile area of Nevada could supply the United States with all its electricity (about 800 gigawatts) using only modestly efficient commercial PV modules.

Myth: Solar energy can solve all of our needs and do everything—at this exact point in time.

Fact: While solar energy is on its way toward becoming a major part of the world's energy portfolio, the industry can't meet all needs at this time. However, it's important now to lay the foundation by making the right investments in solar technology and manufacturing.

Myth: Solar energy cannot significantly offset environmental emissions.

Fact: PV systems produce no atmospheric emissions or greenhouse gases. In fact, when compared to fossil fuel power, each kilowatt of solar electricity annually offsets up to 16 kilograms of nitrogen oxides, 9 kilograms of sulfur oxides, and 2,300 kilograms of carbon dioxide.

Myth: The manufacture of PV is a polluting industry.

Fact: The PV world can't technically take credit for being 100 percent non-polluting, but neither is it a major environmental, safety, or health problem. As far as emissions go from manufacturing, photovoltaics are indeed "cleaner" than fossil fuel sources.

Myth: Solar is a cottage industry that appeals only to smaller niche markets.
Fact: The business of solar shows significant growth each year. The PV industry is expected to grow to a $10 billion–$15 billion per year industry by 2025.

BE IN CHARGE

What to give the gadget-loving person who has everything? Try the solar laptop charger and portable power kit by Earthtech Products. The kit includes a 25-watt "Sunlinq" foldable solar panel and the "XPower Powerpack 300 Plus," which in everyday language means that it can provide up to 300 watts of output of portable electricity and backup power—anywhere. So if you have a friend who's planning a trip to Antarctica or simply wants to get away from it all (but not completely) and needs a working laptop, this might be the perfect gift. The unit provides up to 6 hours of runtime for a 25-watt laptop. For more information, go to **www.earthtechproducts.com.**

COOL OFF WITH THE SUN

Here's something else for the person who has everything: a solar-powered fridge/freezer. The Steca PF 166 refrigerator/freezer runs on a single 70-watt PV module and features a fully programmable temperature control mechanism, automatic voltage detection, and fast cooling due to compressor speed control. For more information, go to **www.stecasolar.com.**

DIY THE SOLAR WAY

If you're looking for a fun weekend (or two) do-it-yourself solar project, consider making a solar heater for less than $500. It can be done, insists Gary Reysa of **www.builditsolar.com.** In fact, he's taken the time make this heater, proving that switching to solar can be surprisingly inexpensive. Reysa provides step-by-step instructions for the project on his website, which are found in the "DIY" section on the home page.

78

AN ALOHA STATE OF MIND

In June 2008, Hawaii governor Linda Lingle signed into law a bill that mandates the installation of solar hot water heating systems in all new single-family homes, beginning in 2010. Her reasoning for the law, the first of its kind in the United States, is solid and visionary: "This solar power legislation is another important step

The fiftieth state relies more heavily on imported fossil fuels than any other state in the nation.

in our long-term plan for energy independence in Hawaii," she told the Associated Press, which also reported that the fiftieth state relies more heavily on imported fossil fuels than any other in the nation. Indeed, state data reveals that approximately 90 percent of Hawaii's energy sources currently come from foreign countries.

In summary, the law mandates that building permits will only be issued if the construction plan includes a solar water heater system. No solar hot water heater = no permit. The rules will be lifted in areas of dense forestation and limited solar gain. Overall, state legislators and renewable energy experts anticipate the law will reduce Hawaii's energy costs by up to 30 percent. Furthermore, according to the Hawaii chapter of the Sierra Club, state leaders have set a goal of 70 percent renewable energy use by 2030.

GETTING TO A BOILING POINT

In addition to generating "clean and green" electricity, solar technology can be applied to generate hot water for your home. The following is a summary of an excellent discussion of solar hot water on the U.S. Department of Energy's Energy Efficiency and Renewable Energy website (**www.eere.energy.gov**).

Also called solar domestic hot water systems, solar water heaters are a cost-effective way to heat the water you use at home. These heaters can be installed and used in a wide range of climates and their fuel (sunshine) costs nothing at all!

Solar hot water heaters are fairly straightforward. They rely on the working relationship forged between storage tanks and solar collectors. Active heaters (versus their passive counter-parts) are equipped with circulating pumps and controls.

You can choose between a two-tank and one-tank installation. Two-tank heating systems work this way: water is preheated in the solar heater and then moved to a conventional water heater. One-tank systems are exactly what they sound like: the solar-heated water is combined with the backup heater.

Residential heaters use a variety of solar collectors, including:

* Flat-Plate Collector: An insulated, weatherproof box that contains a dark absorber plate placed under a glass or plastic cover.

* Integral Collector-Storage Systems: Also called "batch" systems, they have one or more black tanks or tubes in an insulated, glazed box. Unheated water passes through the solar collector and retains that heat gain. The heated water is then sent to the backup heater, where it is stored.

* Evacuated-tube solar collectors: These are installed as parallel rows of transparent glass tubes. Each tube features a glass outer tube and a metal absorber tube attached to something called a "fin," which absorbs solar radiation and prevents heat loss. This type of collector is more commonly used in commercial applications.

To learn (a lot) more, go to the EERE website and search for "solar hot water." There you'll find a wealth of information on solar hot water systems.

80
SOLAR DEGREES

The ad for San Juan College's renewable energy degree program posits a compelling question: "As the sun sets on the age of fossil fuels, where does your future lie?"

The future is indeed bright for those who take their interest in clean energy a step further with a college degree.

Located in sunny Farmington, New Mexico, San Juan College offers a program designed to give students a solid foundation in the fundamental design and installation techniques required to work with renewable technologies. The concentration in photovoltaic system design and installation is offered as an A.A.S. degree or a one-year certificate. The difference between the degree and the certificate is that although both share the same courses, the certificate is for students who already have a degree or who work in a related industry. The degree includes general education courses added to the core content. The program focuses on PV system design and installation, and introduces students to the concepts of wind, micro-hydro, and fuel-cell technology.

For more information about the program and the application process, go to **www.sanjuancollege.edu.**

CAVEAT EMPTOR: SOLAR BEWARE

Make sure you know what you're buying when you decide to install a solar hot water system. The Solar Rating and Certification Corporation (SRCC) provides a certification and rating program for solar hot water collectors, as well as solar water and swimming pool heating systems. For more information, go to **www.solar-rating.org.**

CHECK OUT THESE WHEELS

Evan Tilley, a high school student in Ridgway, a small town in southwestern Colorado a stone's throw from the famous Telluride ski resort, is not the kind of kid who sits around playing video games for fun or watches endless hours of television. Tilley, a soft-spoken young man with a thoughtful, introspective manner, is not willing to let his brain go numb with meaningless activity. Instead, this future creator of computer-generated animation spends his downtime poring over the myriad details of an award-winning solar-powered car, the work of Tilley and the three other solar whiz-kids (Cole McKenzie, Aaron Daughtry, and Stephanie Hanshaw) who comprise the Sunshine Mountain Traveler "Steel Demon" team.

Tilley is the captain of the team, which is led by advisor and sponsor Tom Johnson, who provides the teens with ideas but is not allowed to work on the car. The impetus behind the development of a solar car was to learn the intricacies of solar cells and additional necessary components, such as batteries. The team's car has participated in a variety of races, including one at the Texas Motor Speedway (where it placed fourth out of an international roster of more advanced cars) and the cross-country Dallas-to-Denver excursion, an event that tests both the car and the driver for endurance and creativity should problems arise on the road.

The most important thing is that this three-wheel, scrappy-looking car runs— and it runs the tail off some of the hipper, better-funded designs on the track.

The car travels along at a nice clip of about 10–15 miles per hour. And, to be honest, it doesn't look like much. Parts of it feature that universal holder-together, duct tape. It looks, well, unwieldy. And heavy, very heavy. In fact, it weighs just 1,300 pounds. But the most important thing is that this three-wheel, scrappy-looking car runs—and it runs the tail off some of the hipper, better-funded designs on the track.

Tilley explains that funding is minimal—it's up to the team to raise the cash to keep the car going. [At this writing, the team was up for a potentially significant donation, which would allow for needed improvements to the Steel Demon.] Money goes into materials; for example, a new steering rod and better alignment and suspension tools. The car was built for about $12,000—a rare feat, given that most cars on the winning level cost many times this much. The most expensive components? Batteries, Tilley says.

Tilley's involvement with the team was the result of his strong science background and fascination with the technology that makes a car run on sunshine. Are you inspired to build your own solar-powered vehicle? Tilley offers five tips to help make the job easier:

* Make the car lightweight, otherwise you get too much of what Tilley calls "bad friction"—friction that will cause the car to drag and pull its alignment out of whack.
* Always have an up-to-date wiring diagram on hand in case you need to make a quick fix on the road.
* Take into consideration the weight of the driver: a heavier driver will move the wheels out of alignment, which in turn will create bad friction. Take the time to adjust the alignment each time a new driver sits in the driver's seat. [Tilley's team is currently fundraising to purchase a higher-end alignment system that won't shift.]
* Remember your sprockets! More sprocket teeth can give you a higher speed but will sometimes give you . . . wait for it . . . bad friction. Sometimes fewer sprocket teeth can increase efficiency.
* And finally, keep at it. Says Tilley: "You will have a lot of problems at all times." The message is clear: don't give up. The construction of a solar car should be viewed as a process, not a singular task.

83

SUN, SUN, SUN
YOUR
BOAT

Want to teach your kids about solar technology? Log on to **www.instructables.com** and search for "solar boat." There you'll find detailed instructions for making a toy boat powered by sunshine, as well as many other fun and educational solar projects. Kids are the future; let's work together to get them excited about renewable energy!

FLY THE SOLAR SKIES

Is it a bird? A plane? Well, yes, it's a plane, but what kind of plane? A solar-powered plane? Yes, it's true. Believe!

The Solar Impulse, an ambitious project led by aviation innovators Bertrand Piccard and Andre Borschberg, is now in development and is scheduled to take to the skies for test flights in 2009. The solar-powered aircraft has been designed to promote renewable energy technology and energy efficiency. The creators of the Solar Impulse plan to fly it around the world sans fuel or polluting emissions. The goal is to circumnavigate the globe in 2011, propelled solely by solar energy.

More than an example of extreme technology, the Solar Impulse is meant to be a solar ambassador, spreading the message of the possibilities of renewable energy and getting people excited by the idea of something so unusual finding its wings with rays of sunlight. To learn more, go to **www.solarimpulse.com.**

LIGHTEN UP!

Even solar energy aficionados need to take a break and play a little every now and then. Solar toys are the perfect way to unwind, and you can find numerous kinds, with varying skill levels, at **www.explore4fun.com.** Take a look. Feel the need for a long-lasting flower to place on your office or kitchen windowsill? Then the solar-powered sunflower is made for you. Or, how about a sundial, a solar UFO, a photon solar racecar, or a "sun-print" kit? All can be found on this whimsical website. Take some time and get silly. Saving the planet should be FUN!

FESTIVAL OF BRIGHT IDEAS

Every Memorial Day weekend, the small town of Telluride, Colorado, awakens from its post-ski season downtime to host the annual Mountainfilm Festival, which is, by all accounts, much more than a film festival. In the three decades since its debut, the event has continued to attract bigger and bigger crowds, and along with that its mission has evolved into a multi-faceted strategic goal. In summary, the festival aims to educate and inspire its audience about issues pertaining to a wide range of noteworthy subjects, including conservation/environmental issues/renewable energy (solar, wind, etc.), worldwide culture, mountaineering and other forms of time-honored outdoor exploration, government/policy and, even, the thrill (for some) of shooting down the side of a mountain armed only with two narrow slats composed of high-tech materials beneath one's feet (those would be skis). The eclectic folks who fly, drive, bus, bike, and hitchhike to this former mining town (now A+ ski resort) that sits bumped up against the sheer walls of a formidable box canyon arrive each year ready and eager to learn about how to protect and preserve our precious environment, open up new avenues of understanding between the West and other cultures, and regain a sense of wonderment in the natural world. For more information, go to **www.mountainfilm.org.**

SOLAR APPEAL

Good news for the 2008 Solar Power International convention and trade show held in San Diego, California: a record 20,000 people (20 percent of whom were from outside the United States) showed up to learn about the latest and greatest in the rapidly advancing arena of solar technology. Sponsored by the Solar Electric Power Association and the Solar Energy Industries· Association, the convention has grown from 60 exhibitors in 2003 to 425 in 2008. The 2009 event will accommodate some 800 exhibitors.

88

SOLAR . . . CEMETERIES?

Talk about unusually innovative! The town of Santa Coloma de Gramenet, near Barcelona, recently installed 462 grid-tied solar panels atop the mausoleums in its cemetery. And why did they do this, you might be thinking? Seems the town was eager to embrace solar technology but couldn't find any unoccupied land

In a moment of life-changing *ah ha!*, the creative and scientific minds behind the project turned their attention to the town's cemetery—it sits on flat, open land and gets plenty of sun. It was, in all respects, the perfect place.

that met the main criteria of a successful solar array: open and flat, and with excellent year-round sun exposure. In fact, Santa Coloma is so packed that its 124,000 residents barely manage to squeeze themselves into the one-and-a-half-square-mile city boundary. In a moment of life-changing *ah ha!*, the creative and scientific minds behind the project turned their attention to the town's cemetery—it sits on flat, open land and gets plenty of sun. It was, in all respects, the perfect place. Well, except for the fact that it is a cemetery.

It was not a popular plan at first. Opponents worried that a solar array would disrespect the peaceful resting place of the deceased. In response, town hall and cemetery officials embarked on a widespread public relations campaign to convince wary folks that the project was worthy of such placement, and that it would be installed and maintained with tender, loving care and, most of all, respect for those who had left this world.

The solar panels, which sit atop the mausoleums, face due south and produce as much energy as the annual consumption of 60 single-family homes. The electricity feeds into the local power grid and is expected to prevent some 62 tons of carbon dioxide from entering the atmosphere.

Says Esteve Serret, director of Conste-Live Energy, the renewable energy company that runs the solar cemetery, "The best tribute we can pay to our ancestors, whatever your religion may be, is to generate clean energy for new generations. That is our leitmotif."

89 LIGHTING THE PATH

In 2008, *U.S. News and World Report* named Amory Lovins, co-founder of the Rocky Mountain Institute, one of "America's Best Leaders." The honor is apropos for a man who, as the magazine points out, " . . . has been arguing—in journals, at conferences, to big-name CEOs and Pentagon officials, and, for that matter, anyone who will listen—that the inefficient use of natural resources is one of the main culprits behind the country's energy problems."

But Lovins is not necessarily all about building a brigade of happy "green" people. He approaches the quest for renewable sources of energy like a businessman views the bottom line: if it's not economically feasible and satisfying, it's not going to capture the minds and hearts of those being asked to make the break from fossil fuels. Show people they can make money with renewables, Lovins posits, and they will more likely stand up and take notice.

The Colorado-based Rocky Mountain Institute has headquarters in Snowmass and another office in downtown Boulder. RMI calls itself a "think and do" tank, and its founder is something of an eccentric, a big-brained scientist trained as a physicist at Harvard and Oxford who then went on to follow his passion of making renewable energy and energy efficiency key solutions to global warming, or, as he puts it, "global weirding." Long an advocate for solar-generated electricity, the bane of his existence is that so much of the empty roof space in this country is not put toward an eco-conscious use when those acres and acres of surface could be used to support PV panels.

RMI is an independent, entrepreneurial, nonprofit organization, and it aims for its work to have a "strong emphasis on market-based solutions." For more information, go to **www.rmi.org.** Be sure to check out the online tour of the headquarters facility, which features everything from a solar hot water system to a fully functioning greenhouse with pond.

CHARGE IT WITH SOLAR

The folks at *Real Goods* have done it again by offering a gadget that, once learned about, becomes one of those must-have devices. Their Universal Solar Charger is, the company says, the "lightest, fastest solar charger on the market." This handy unit delivers a straight charge to portable electronics lacking in juice: iPod, Blackberry, and cell phone (Nokia, Samsung, Sony, Ericsson, Siemens, or Motorola). It's easy to use, too: just unfold it, connect the mini USB cord with the proper adapter tip, and your device will be fully charged in two to three hours of direct sunlight. For more information, go to **www.realgoods.com** and search for "Universal Solar Charger."

GET ACTIVE!

My hope is that you are ready to take direct action to encourage your local and/or state government to make serious steps toward a solar-powered future. Activism is all fine and dandy, but where to start? Here are some ways to begin volunteering for the planet:

* Start a renewable energy "support group" at which you and others concerned about the nation's current dependence on

fossil fuels can brainstorm strategies for reaching the people who can make a difference.

* The Solar Energy Industries Association (SEIA) needs your support if you are or plan to become a professional working in the field of renewables. Make it a point to participate in SEIA events at state and regional levels. To learn more about SEIA, go to **www.seia.org.**

* Write a letter to your state representative expressing your views about solar energy and what you would like to see happen in your state.

* Learn as much as you can. Read books. Surf the Internet. Talk to professionals about what they envision for the future.

* Make your green vote count; at times you might have to cross party lines to vote for the candidate who has the best interests of the planet at heart.

* Offer to be a clearinghouse of sorts for people who want to know about renewable energy. Share the information you have gathered (of course respecting copyrights, but some information, including that posted on the U.S. Department of Energy website, for example, is free to the public).

* Hold a solar fund-raiser. Donate the money to an eco-minded organization in your area, or choose a national nonprofit and send them a check.

* Write opinion letters to your local newspaper, or volunteer to write a column about the environment, if you have the time and feel comfortable putting your writing out there for public scrutiny. If you don't yet feel comfortable publishing your writing, ask a writer-friend to help you organize your thoughts.

92

MAKING RAISINS IN THE SUN

The health benefits of a diet rich in whole foods, versus their processed counterparts, are increasingly evident. Sometimes, however, the hectic pace of modern life can make it difficult to find nutrient-filled snacks and the tendency is to grab whatever might be available at the time (we shudder to think!).

Dried fruits and vegetables fit the bill as worthy snacks, and having them around is a wise idea. And, because this is a book about solar energy, guess what: some very bright and innovative folks determined to be hands-on with their food have engineered special dehydrators that operate on nothing but good old-fashioned sunshine.

A detailed explanation (along with photos) of solar food dehydrators is available at **www.geopathfinder.com** (click on the "Food Preservation" link on the left-side menu). I recommend you take the time to read through the fascinating explanation of and instructions for this tummy-friendly technology. Building a solar dehydrator would be a perfect weekend project for teaching kids about the benefits of renewable energy and also to give them an intimate look at how food is produced (no, it doesn't always come in plastic packages with zip-tight fasteners).

The website lists the basics of a solar dehydrator:

* Glazing (glass or greenhouse plastics);
* Black surface over the food (metal or fabric);
* Food-safe screen to hold food;
* Corrugated, galvanized metal roofing tilted toward the sun.

Here's how it works: sunlight goes through the clear glazing and hits the black surface, heating it. This heat then radiates from the black surface to the food screen below. The sloped metal roofing on which everything rests reflects heat back up toward the food, and its corrugations act as crucial airspace beneath the screen for allowing "bad" humid air to escape via natural convection.

For even more in-depth reading, check out *A Pantry Full of Sunshine* by Larisa Walk, who, with partner Robert A. Dahse, owns and operates the Geopathfinder website. This book and others are available for purchase on the site. By the way, it's obvious that Walk and Dahse know their stuff: they have lived off the grid for more than 25 years, and they grow all of their own food.

SUN BATHING

I'd like to tell you a personal story now. Some time ago, during my adventurous twenties, I traveled to the Everest region of Nepal to volunteer at a high-altitude treatment clinic that served trekkers, mountaineers on their way to scale the highest peak on the planet, and those who helped get them there: the Sherpas and the porters. The clinic was . . . well, let's just say it was *rustic*. Light came from candles, heat from several creaky, barely working kerosene lanterns. The act of getting warm water was an hours-long process. To begin with, you had to carry it in from a nearby river in a heavy, tarnished metal pot. Then that pot had to sit above a meager flame until, a long while later, little bubbles began to announce the presence of something divine and sublime: water about to boil.

There was no shower, and everyone in the clinic wore extra layers of fleece to disguise their body odor. (I didn't say this story would be pretty.) On sunny days, those intrepid enough to withstand freezing temperatures in the name of being clean (I

I can recall, clearly, how it felt to take my first solar shower in the Nepali Khumbu, at the base of Everest, a mountain so tall it forms its own jet stream. I had not properly bathed in what seemed like a month. I had washcloth-bathed, yes, but I craved the feel of warm water sliding down my tired, altitude-weary body.

wasn't one of them) would allow themselves to be doused with water from a nearby creek as they scrubbed with eco-friendly soap, frantically, hurried, as in, "What I am thinking, doing this?" They turned slightly blue all right—but they were *clean*.

Then something downright celebratory happened. A generous soul gifted a solar shower to the clinic. It was easy to use: Fill it with water upon rising early in the morning and hang it outside in full sun until the water in its black bag heated up. Its design was simple and yet clever: a heavy-duty vinyl bag, a hook to support the bag, and a dangling hose with a showerhead terminus for gentle and even water flow. Bliss.

I can recall, clearly, how it felt to take my first solar shower in the Nepali Khumbu, at the base of Everest, a mountain so tall it forms its own jet stream. I had not properly bathed in what seemed like a month. I had washcloth-bathed, yes, but I craved the feel of warm water sliding down my tired, altitude-weary body. I remember the giddy anticipation of stepping under the black bag, my privacy secured by a makeshift shower stall consisting of two ancient pieces of sheet metal propped up against each other, and releasing the spigot, allowing the water to flow.

And it was hot! So hot, so good. I quickly washed my waist-length hair, unwound it from its tight braid, thrilled to the goosebumps on my skin as a breeze kicked up.

And then, this wonderful adventure turned into Hell. A vicious "100-year blizzard," as the locals call them, swept through the region, burying people and livestock and destroying entire villages with a series of unrelenting avalanches that roared down the mountainsides like freight trains. Go back to November 1995, if you like, and Google it. Trekkers, climbers, porters, Sherpas, local villagers—all stumbled into the tiny stone clinic, desperate for medicine, a helicopter ride to the relative sanity of the city, a cure, however unrealistic, for feet, hands, eyeballs, even knees frostbitten beyond repair. The trekking paths lay buried beneath four feet of snow, heavy as cement, the only passage narrow, tunnel-like intrusions created by brave locals and the yaks that had managed to survive. It turned dark in that corner of the world, and the solar shower was put away. People were dying. There was work to do. But the memories of my time there, some good but most of them sad, angry, and still unresolved, do include the few times I bathed in water warmed by the golden Himalayan sun. And as I get older and wiser (gulp!), I now see that this is the way of life: The sublime moments line up next to the somber times, the days of abundance give way to restriction and closure.

So, dear readers, thank you for indulging me. All of this was my way of saying: Go buy an outdoor solar shower. Don't wait to go camping or trekking or fishing or mountain biking or boating or cross country skiing to use it. Hang it up in your yard, even, let the sun work its infinite magic, and feel just how close you are to nature, to the Earth.

A LITTLE LIGHT READING

These magazines and journals are excellent sources of information about renewable energy. *Mother Earth News, Home Power, Dwell, Popular Science, National Geographic, Fast Company, E: The Environmental Magazine, Solar Today* (publication of the American Solar Energy Society).

ENLIGHTENING BOOKS

Bookstores and online book retailers such as Amazon and Barnes and Noble provide plenty of options for consumers seeking information on renewable energy solutions, sustainability, and green living. In order to help you navigate the offerings, I've done some of the legwork for you. Here are a few of my favorites, in no particular order:

The Complete Idiot's Guide to Solar Power for your Home,
by Dan Ramsey with David Hughes (Alpha, a member of the Penguin Group (USA), Inc., second edition, 2007).

The Solar Electric House: Energy for the Environmentally Responsive Energy-Independent Home, by Steven J. Strong and William G. Scheller (Sustainability Press, 1994).

The Solar House: Passive Heating and Cooling, by Daniel D. Chiras (Chelsea Green Publishing Company, 2002).

It's Easy Being Green, by Crissy Trask (Gibbs Smith, Publisher, 2006).

Go Green: How to Build an Earth-Friendly Community, by Nancy H. Taylor (Gibbs Smith, Publisher, 2008).

Green Living: The E Magazine Handbook for Living Lightly on the Earth, by the editors of E/The Environmental Magazine (Plume, published by the Penguin Group, 2005).

Solar Energy Projects for the Evil Genius: 50 Build-It-Yourself Projects, by Gavin D.J. Harper (McGraw-Hill, 2007).

Sunracing, by Richard and Melissa King (Human Resource Development Press, 1993).

Cooking with the Sun, by Beth Halacy (Morning Sun Press, 1992).

Solar Cooking for Home and Camp, by Linda Frederick Yaffe (Stackpole Books, 2007).

Cradle to Cradle: Remaking the Way We Make Things, by William McDonough and Michael Braungart (North Point Press, a division of Farrar, Straus and Giroux, 2002).

The Passive Solar House, by James Kachadorian (Chelsea Green Publishing Company, 2006).

A Golden Thread: 2,500 Years of Solar Architecture and Technology, by Ken Butti and John Perlin (Cheshire Books, 1980).

The Easy Guide to Solar Electric, by Adi Pieper (ADI Solar, 2007).

Eco-Women: Protectors of the Earth, by Willow Ann Sirch (Fulcrum Publishing, 2009).

SOLID STIRLING

"Creating a brighter future for humanity through solar energy."

That's the stated goal of Stirling Energy Systems. The company has developed what it calls the SunCatcher, a 25-kW solar power system that tracks the sun and focuses solar energy onto a powerful conversion unit. This in turn converts the heat to "grid-quality electricity."

The SunCatcher combines a mirrored concentrator dish with a high-efficiency Stirling engine specially designed to convert sunlight to electricity. What's most compelling about SunCatchers is that they DO NOT employ photovoltaics. SES states that PV technology is not yet "abundant enough or cost-effective enough to meet any large-scale demands."

The SunCatcher solar dish is similar in shape to a large satellite (approximately 38 inches in diameter) and clad in curved mirrors. The dishes are programmed to face the sun and focus that energy on a collector. The collector is in turn connected to a Stirling engine, which takes that thermal power and uses it to heat hydrogen in a closed-loop system. From there, expanding hydrogen gas forms a pressure wave on the pistons of the engine, which spins an electric motor, generating electricity with no fuel cost or pollution. "This technology is referred to as solar thermal or concentrating solar power," the company explains.

The current market for the SunCatcher is utility-scale power generation versus small-scale residential or commercial use.

As of this writing, SES was in the process of developing two solar sites in California. Referred to as Solar 1 and Solar 2, these two phases are "significant first steps in deploying large-scale renewable solar technology as a commercial energy project. When fully completed, both sites will have a combined generating capacity of 1,750 MW," the company says. Imagine: thousands of SunCatchers doing their part to feed electricity to the grid.

To learn more about this amazingly innovative company, go to **www.stirlingenergy.com.**

SUNSHINE IN A BOTTLE

The waterproof, frosted glass "Sun Jar" by Tobias Wong captures sunshine and stores it for use at night. Each jar contains a small solar power cell and a rechargeable battery to provide about 5 hours of grid-free light. The soft glow that emits from the jar rivals any candlelight for peaceful, cozy ambiance. Available at **www.inhabit.com, www.charlesandmarie.com,** and other Internet retailers. Retail price: $44.

IN PRAISE OF FRESH AIR

Is the interior of your car feeling a little stuffy these days? Are you not keen to leave your windows rolled down—even a smidge—to allow fresh air in while you are away from your vehicle? Not to worry: Earthtech Products makes a solar-powered automobile vent, aptly named the AutoVent SPV, that runs on solar energy and keeps that closed-in environment fresh and free of hot, stale air, humidity, and pet odors. Installation is quick and easy: attach the included weatherproof strips to the ventilator, then place it on top of the window edge and close the window. The unit exchanges the air every 20 minutes. At this writing, the gadget was on sale for $29.99—which is inexpensive enough to give it a try. Could this become a favorite stocking stuffer?

A BOOK YOU SHOULD READ

Am I actually advising you, dear reader, to purchase a book other than mine? Yes, I am. Very much so. And here's why: *The 30th Anniversary Real Goods Solar Living Source Book* is a true marvel. Edited by John Schaeffer and published by Gaiam Real Goods, the 634-page tome is thankfully in paperback, otherwise it might be too heavy to lift. Here's what *Real Goods* has to say about its masterpiece: "(It) is the ultimate resource on renewable energy, sustainable living, alternative construction, green building, homesteading, off-the-grid living and alternative transportation."

I'm happy to recommend it. It's a nice bookend to *Turn Me On*. Consider the former a fresh, light appetizer. Then comes *Real Goods* — a hearty meal filled with every nutrient you'd ever want.

IT ALL COMES DOWN TO 1: YOU

This book is essentially a list of 100 ways to get excited about solar power. Coming up with this list was no small task. With solar technology gaining momentum at what seems like breakneck speed, finding the right balance of information to present within these pages was a challenge.

And then I arrived at #100. What could I say to end this book, how would I wrap up the information contained in items 1–99? The solution came to me easily: of course, I must celebrate the reader!

Without folks like you, those who are willing to dip their toes into the ever deepening and widening pool that is solar technology, the future would not look nearly as bright.

Without folks like you, those who are willing to dip their toes into the ever deepening and widening pool that is solar technology, the future would not look nearly as bright. True change comes from a shift in mass thinking. The only way we can save our planet is by encouraging each and every person to somehow care about saving our planet. We do not have to become experts on this sweeping topic. We do not have to necessarily understand exactly how sunlight can be channeled to power our toasters and coffeemakers. What we DO need is a collective passion for change. We desperately need a new way of thinking about how we consume our natural resources and how we can mitigate the effects of a too-long dependence on fossil fuels.

Each morning, the sun is there to greet us as we rise to meet the day. Will that sun solve every last problem we've ever considered? No. But that sun holds endless possibilities, and that you have taken the time to understand the basics of those possibilities is an accomplishment you should be proud of.

And so I say, thank you, #100, the reader who decided to care.

INDEX

A

AC, 30, 33, 41, 85
active solar, 17, 95
activism, 132–133
aesthetics, 88
air-conditioning, 57, 64, 87
airplane, 125
alternating current, *see AC*
amorphous, 25, 73–74
attached, 28

B

backup, 30
battery, 16, 41, 44, 84, 142
  capacity, 34
  lead-acid, 34–35
  overcharging, 17
bicycle, 77
biomimicry, 66
boat, 125
breakers, 41

C

camping, 27, 85, 97, 138
carbon, 13
  emissions, *see emissions*
  saved, 91
carbon dioxide, 13–15, 19, 63, 129
cemeteries, 128
charge controller, 16–17, 35, 41
charger, 114, 132
clean energy, 19, 37, 70, 113, 118

climate change, 13–15
clothes dryers, 109–110
coal-fired power plant, 19, 39
coffee, 81–82
collector, 141
combiner, 41
components, 41
conferences, 53, 92
contractor, 40, 92
conventions, 127
cooking, 63, 97–100, 135
cool, 74
cooler, 63
cost, 27, 43, 45, 103
current, 17

D

DC, 25, 30, 33–34, 41, 85
dehydrators, 135
direct current, *see DC*
direct gain, 23
direct sunlight, 108

E

ecological consequences, 14
education, 88, 104–105, 120, 125
electricity, 16, 27, 113, 129
  installations, 104–105
  production, 76, 118, 141–142
  selling, 29
  usage, 88–91
electrolyte, 35, 76

ORGANIZATIONS, BUSINESSES, PRODUCTS

NOTES

NOTES

NOTES

NOTES

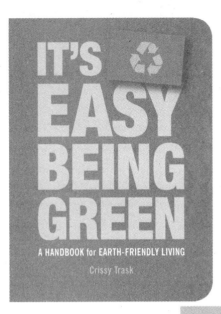

COT DEATH: *The Facts*

COT DEATH

The Facts

Jane Chumbley

WARD LOCK

A WARD LOCK BOOK

First published in the UK 1997
by Ward Lock
Wellington House
125 Strand
LONDON
WC2R 0BB

A Cassell Imprint

ISBN 0 7063 7433 9
Designed by Paula McCann
Printed and bound in Great Britain by Mackays of Chatham

CONTENTS

ACKNOWLEDGEMENTS

I would like to thank the staff at the Foundation for the Study of Infant Deaths for their help in tracking down many of the relevant papers and for commenting on the manuscript.

Note: Nobody can agree how we should refer to mixed gender groups such as babies, so I haven't followed any particular convention. Where it doesn't seem pedantic I've written 'he or she'. At other times I've opted for a single pronoun. No gender bias is intended.

Chapter One

INTRODUCTION

'Jane went in to wake him up and I heard her scream. I ran in and he was cold, lying on his stomach. I took him, laid him on the floor and tried to revive him while Jane phoned the ambulance. I kept trying until they took him to hospital where he was pronounced dead. But I already knew that . . . It's a bit like cancer. You're aware of it, but it's never going to happen to you.'

Cot death is every new parent's worst nightmare. Few people can be left untouched by the death of a baby or young child in whatever circumstances. There seems to be no logic, no sense to it, that a life should be created only to end so soon. For parents, the loss of a baby is the end of a dream and nothing will ever be the same again. That the loss in cot death is so sudden, so unexpected and so inexplicable only accentuates their shock and disbelief. With cot death there's no warning, no build-up and no time to anticipate and fear the worst. You could say there's no chance to say goodbye.

Knowing and fearing cot death can cast a shadow over the birth of a new baby. First time parents are particularly vulnerable. For them, everything is new and the sense of responsibility can be overwhelming. It's not surprising if parents check, check and check again while their baby is sleeping during those first few days and weeks.

This book has been written to give you the facts about cot

death – to bring you up to date with what doctors know, and
what they don't know. It will tell you what there is to know
about reducing the risk of cot death. Cot death is relatively rare
these days and, thanks to new advice on prevention, it seems
to be getting more uncommon. But the problem hasn't gone
away. Every week nine or ten babies die of cot death. Tragedy
does strike and no-one is to blame. If someone you know suffers
a cot death, this book will help you to understand some of the
emotions they may be feeling. More importantly, the information it provides could make you a better friend and comforter.

The Mystery

Cot death outrages and affronts us because we live in an age of
spectacular medical advances. We're used to medical science
finding answers and solving problems. Somehow it doesn't
seem right that a baby can just slip away and die and no-one
knows why. For a couple whose baby has died of cot death, the
mystery compounds the agony.

We also live in a blame culture, and you only have to watch
the news for a week to see that it's parents who are often the
targets when officials are apportioning blame for society's woes.
But so far as cot death is concerned, blame just isn't an issue. It
may be a natural response for parents to blame themselves, and
it's possible there are things they could have done to reduce the
risk of their baby dying of cot death – such as following advice
to give up smoking. But babies die of cot death when there are
no obvious risk factors, and not only is it morally wrong, but it's
also literally impossible to state, for example, that a woman's
smoking during pregnancy **caused** her baby to die of cot death.
No-one knows what **causes** cot death – all we know about is
risk factors: things which seem, on the balance of the evidence
available, to make cot death more likely.

Thankfully these days fewer people than ever believe that

cot death is the result of infanticide or think that babies have died 'in suspicious circumstances'. But where such attitudes do persist they are an intolerable injustice to grief-stricken parents. A coroner's investigation is required whenever the doctor can't give a cause of death and government statistics for 1989 show that in over 98 per cent of these cases the coroner was satisfied there was no evidence of homicide.

The Time and the Place

'Cot death' is a catch-all term which gives a name to what happens when a baby dies suddenly and unexpectedly. Actually, it's a bit misleading, since it suggests that the victims always die in cots, with the implication that the deaths take place during the night. In fact, cot deaths can happen at any time and in any place. One of the largest studies of the past five years found that two thirds of deaths were discovered between 5am and 10am. But if they hadn't been checked since they were set down, the babies could have died at any time during the night or early morning. A series of studies of babies who died of cot death in the 1970s and early 1980s regularly found that over half died between 9am and 9pm. Babies have died of 'cot death' whilst in the car, at the childminder's or nursery, or even while held in their mother's arms.

And cot death isn't something new. It's not an invention of the twentieth century, although it's only in the last century or so that it has been taken seriously as a medical problem in need of research and investigation. No, cot death has been around for thousands of years. It even seems to have been mentioned in the Bible: 'And when I rose in the morning to give my child suck, behold it was dead' (I Kings 3:21, King James version) – although in this case the death was attributed to 'overlaying' as were many subsequent infant deaths.

The history of cot death is littered with theories, interpretations, wrong turns and U-turns. In the late eighteenth and early nineteenth centuries, doctors believed that an enlarged thymus was to blame and it was thought that this could interfere with the normal working of the heart and lungs. But in 1842 someone pointed out that the small thymus normally seen in babies who died of other causes was invariably shrunken because of chronic disease so that the apparently enlarged thymus in cot death babies was in fact entirely normal size.

Infanticide, accidental smothering, spasms of the larynx, streptococcal infection, inhalation of vomit, allergy to cow's milk, respiratory disease, vitamin and mineral deficiencies, low blood sugar and excess sodium in the blood – all of these have had their season as explanations for the apparently inexplicable. Historically, advice on prevention has been pretty thin on the ground, but has included irradiation of the thymus gland (which actually then caused cancer of the thymus), putting the baby to bed in a separate cot, avoiding soft pillows and postponing bottlefeeding for at least two weeks after birth.

It wasn't until the second half of the twentieth century that cot death was given a name and recognised as a syndrome. Research in the past few decades has focused on pathology, physiology, epidemiology and prevention:

◇ Pathology: closer attention to the post mortem means that in a few cases a cause of death has been identified – an inherited metabolic disorder, for example. Post mortem examinations can also help to support or disprove a theory.

◇ Physiology: we now know more than ever about the way babies develop both in the womb and in the first six months of life – how their breathing develops, how their heart rate changes, what happens in the young brain and so on. Through this it is possible to detect where things may be going wrong, or when a baby may be particularly vulnerable to outside influences.

◇ Epidemiology: by studying healthy babies alongside those who have died of cot death it is possible to work out what may or may not be relevant risk factors.
◇ Prevention: once a potential risk factor has been identified, researchers can study what happens when one group of parents changes their behaviour to eliminate the risk.

A Cautious Approach

Studies so far have revealed a lot. But researchers today are very cautious about making pronouncements on cot death and governments perhaps even more so. So far as the doctors and scientists doing the research and the charity funding much of the research – the Foundation for the Study of Infant Deaths (FSID) – are concerned, there is a reluctance to jump the gun, to give advice on the basis of a single study or even a number of studies in which there are some design flaws. This is the case at the moment with breastfeeding. In New Zealand, breastfeeding is included as one of the major preventative factors in campaigning. In the UK, there has been no concrete evidence to support the idea that breastfeeding reduces the risk of cot death. So whilst doctors and the Foundation will happily recommend breastfeeding for its many advantages, they can't with hand on heart say it will help to prevent cot death – not yet, at least (see Chapter 7). There's a fundamental honesty and scrupulous attention to detail underpinning the desire simply to 'get it right' and to be certain that any advice to parents does no harm.

On the other hand, it may be hard for the parents of babies who died of cot death in 1990 or 1991 and who had been put to bed on their tummies to accept that they couldn't have been warned earlier of the very real risk this poses. By the late 1980s the risk of sleeping prone (on the tummy) had been spotted in several studies, but it's always easy to say with hindsight that the evidence was conclusive. It was studies which observed what happened when groups of people changed the way they put their babies to bed that finally settled the risk as real and substantial. These studies are outlined in Chapter 4. Ironically, despite all the evidence, in the US there is still a marked reluctance among officials to endorse the advice about sleeping position, possibly for fear of litigation. Writing in the *Lancet* about a New Zealand study which seemed to show a reduced risk of cot death amongst babies who shared a room with adults (see Chapter 8), Professor Peter Pharoah from the Department of Public Health at the University of Liverpool said this:

'I believe the recommendation made by the New Zealand group – that infants should sleep in the same bedroom as their parents – is not adequately justified by the evidence presented so far. In the recent controversy over the progestogen component of oral contraceptives, the statement was made that academics were prone to light the touch paper and then stand back. Epidemiological evidence always needs close scrutiny, especially before pundits expound advice to parents on such an emotive subject as sudden infant death.'

These arguments are, of course, particularly applicable to the debate about cot mattresses and their role, if any, in cot death (see Chapter 9).

The Incidence of Cot Death

In the UK, all but 8 out of every 1000 babies born alive live to see their first birthday. Of those who do not survive, the majority die because they are born too soon and are too small. Some die because they are born with a fatal abnormality, some because of infection, a few of cancer or a rare condition. One baby in 1670 dies of cot death.

In the past seven years the number of cot deaths in the UK has fallen by 70 per cent – from over 1500 to under 500 (see the following graph). 'Sudden and unexpected death in infancy' became a registrable cause of death in 1971. Before that, a lot of cot deaths were probably registered as 'sudden respiratory deaths at home'. If you add together the figures for these two causes of death it seems probable that the cot death rate was fairly constant at around 2.0–2.3 per 1000 live births for at least a couple of decades before the recent dramatic drops. The cot death rate in the UK now stands at 0.6 per 1000 live births – that's equivalent to one baby out of every 1670. In practical terms, it's nine or ten babies a week.

To put things in perspective, cot death is the most common cause of death in babies over one month old. There are more cot deaths than there are deaths from cancer among children under the age of 15. (Official statistics on cot death exclude figures for children aged over 12 months.)

Cot Deaths in the UK Among Babies up to One Year

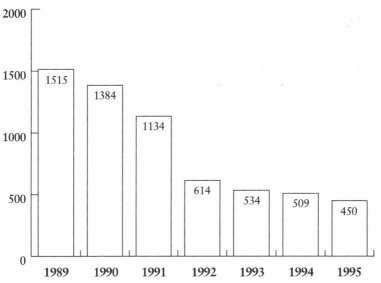

International Picture

Cot death is an international problem, but comparing one country's cot death rate with that of another isn't straightforward because of differences in the way cot deaths are reported and classified, and because not all countries do post mortems on babies who die suddenly. So there's simply no guarantee that you're comparing like with like. Historically, though, it has been useful to make the comparison because it can highlight differences in childcare practices which might increase the risk of cot death. For example, researchers have been particularly interested in New Zealand which has had a very high rate of cot death in the past, and in Hong Kong where the cot death rate is extremely low. Within New Zealand there were marked differences in the incidence of cot death among different communities – lowest among the South Sea Islanders who almost invariably place their babies on their backs to sleep, for example. The cot death rate in the UK is similar to that of other industrialised countries, most of which have seen a considerable fall in rates over the past five or six years. (In the following table, not all figures are from the same year.)

Recent Cot Death Rates (per 1000 live births)

Australia	1.0
Austria	1.2
Belgium	1.72
Canada	0.82
Denmark	0.3
England & Wales	0.6*
Finland	0.6
France	1.8
Germany	2.5
Hong Kong	0.3

Ireland – Republic	0.7
– Northern	1.45
Italy	2.6
Japan	0.31
Netherlands	0.35
New Zealand	1.4
Norway	0.8
Scotland	1.31
Sweden	0.5
USA	1.4

(Compiled by Ms Kaaren Fitzgerald for SIDRF and
the Global Strategy Task Force, June 1995, *except for
more recent figure for England & Wales, from Office
for National Statistics Monitor DH3 96/2.)

Taking Action

The good news about cot death is that in some cases prevention may be possible. Taking action is vital – not only because it may save a baby's life, but also because it may be a very small consolation for those parents who do suffer a cot death. It's almost certain that these parents will feel guilty and that they will search for things they could have done to prevent their baby dying. Knowing they have done all the 'right' things won't ease the anger or pain of a tragic bereavement but it may prevent them blaming themselves or each other for the rest of their lives.

The expert advice to parents on sleeping position, smoking, temperature control, breastfeeding, mattresses, room sharing, bed sharing and dealing with illness is explored in detail in Chapters 4 to 9. The great thing about this advice is that for the most part it is extremely simple and practical. It doesn't require a scientific background, medical qualifications or nursing experience. It's advice that all parents can follow from the day their baby is born. The advice to give up smoking is obviously harder to achieve, but far from condemning parents who smoke, understanding health professionals will give these parents as much support as they possibly can to help them quit or reduce the baby's exposure to smoke.

In order to give a full picture of the situation as it stands, many of the following chapters contain statistics and research details. It isn't vital that you remember any of these things and the key facts are summarised at the end of each chapter. Cot death is complicated and it can be frightening, but arming yourself with the facts means you can reduce the risks.

Chapter Two

WHAT IS COT DEATH?

Most people would probably define cot death as the sudden, unexpected and unexplained death of a baby or very young child – or something along those lines. Unfortunately, when it comes to collecting and coding information from death certificates, it's never quite that simple and there have been various twists and turns in the terms and definitions used over the last 40 or 50 years.

The term cot death was first used in 1954 by a Dr A. M. Barrett, a Cambridge pathologist. He used it to describe cases in which 'an apparently healthy infant is unexpectedly found dead in its sleeping quarters'. A decade later this definition was amended slightly to incorporate the idea that, medically speaking, the death couldn't be explained. From now on, 'cot death' would be used as a cause of death when the post mortem revealed no clues and no other diagnosis would fit. (Although, very occasionally, doctors do register a second or even third cause of death on the certificate – see Chapter 3.)

It wasn't until 1971 that the Registrar General and the Coroners' Society of England and Wales agreed that 'sudden or unexpected death in infancy' should be a registrable cause of death. The term sudden infant death syndrome (SIDS) wasn't introduced into the international coding system until 1979. These days a cot death may be registered as SIDS, sudden or unexpected death in infancy, sudden infant death or, indeed, cot death. In this book, the terms cot death and SIDS are used interchangeably.

A Mystery

Whatever you call it – sudden infant death syndrome, SIDS or cot death – it can't be explained in medical terms. A baby stops breathing and there's nothing the post mortem examination can find to help us understand why. It's a popular misconception that cot death is something to do with suffocation. A baby might appear to have suffocated because he or she is found face down or fully covered in bedding, but death due to suffocation is thought to be rare. We don't even know if the babies die because they stop breathing, or if they stop breathing because they are dead: in a post mortem it's not possible to see whether the airway collapsed during life or not.

In cot death, babies just seem to slip away. People have said it is just as if a light has been switched off – and there is some evidence to suggest that in some cases the death can be as sudden and as silent as that. Early research published in the US in 1972 found that despite the fact that an adult was sleeping in the same room in 31 per cent of cases, no-one reported hearing any noise such as crying.

Initially, when you approach a baby who has died of cot death, there may be no obvious signs that anything is wrong or unusual. It is quite normal for babies to be extremely still when they sleep. Unless they have a blocked nose or enlarged tonsils, they usually breathe so quietly and are so still in sleep that to start with new parents often feel they have to touch their baby to check he or she is still alive. But a baby who has died of cot death will be very pale and there may be other signs that something has happened, such as blood stains on the bedclothes, blood-tinged froth around the mouth or blotchy red or purple marks on the skin. These are signs that death has occurred – not problems which have caused or contributed to the death. The blood-tinged froth is caused by pulmonary oedema – a sort of congestion in the lungs – which happens after death as the body systems shut down and some of the air in the lungs slowly passes out taking fluid with it. The blotches occur because there is no blood flow after death and so some blood seeps out of the vessels at the lowest point. Where the blotches occur will depend on the position the baby is lying in.

Apparent Life Threatening Events (ALTEs)

Although we don't know if cot death is the result of a baby stopping breathing, this has obviously been a popular area for research. In fact, it's quite normal for babies to stop breathing for a few seconds – even up to 15 or 20 seconds – and it's not something that will do them any harm. These pauses are brief episodes of apnoea – a medical term which means that air flow into the lungs has stopped. Apnoea can be the result of an obstruction in the windpipe or it may be that breathing movements have just stopped temporarily. It's now quite widely known that adult snorers may suffer from sleep apnoea – their airways are blocked by the fatty tissue in the neck and they may stop breathing for a few seconds before waking suddenly. This can happen literally hundreds of times during the night.

If apnoea is more prolonged, it can cause what's called an Apparent (or Acute) Life Threatening Event (ALTE). The pause in breathing leads to a sudden drop in the amount of oxygen in the blood. This in turn makes the skin turn blue or white and the baby may go floppy, choke, gag or become very stiff and stare blankly. ALTEs are extremely frightening and there's often no reason why they occur and no warning that they are about to happen. Sometimes they might be linked to an infection or caused by a baby inhaling vomit, but it has been calculated that only 4 to 10 per cent are caused by an obstruction in the airway. Some babies have repeat attacks, others don't. One study found that problems with the central nervous system were responsible in 7 out of 46 cases (15 per cent) but that in 4 out of the 7 cases nobody had suspected a problem beforehand.

A baby can suffer an ALTE and start breathing independently. But, if you witness an ALTE, you're obviously not going to wait for this to happen: the important thing is to do something to get the baby to breathe again normally. Shaking, pinching or flicking the soles of the feet might stimulate breathing, or you may need to start mouth-to-mouth resuscitation (see Chapter 12).

Special baby monitors – called apnoea monitors – have been designed to detect any pauses in a baby's breathing pattern. These are used in a programme for parents who have already suffered a cot death and are worried about the safety of subsequent babies. But there's no evidence to prove that these kinds of monitors reduce the incidence of cot death. In fact, a UK survey in 1989 found that 16 per cent of paediatricians questioned had a baby patient die while the parents were using a monitor. By 1993 at least 64 babies had died in these circumstances. In the US the widespread use of monitors has not produced a fall in the cot death rate. Chapter 12 contains more details about apnoea monitors.

Nobody knows if apnoea is the cause of cot death or whether a baby who suffers an ALTE is at greater risk of cot death. Like cot death, ALTEs are more common in boys, premature babies and babies under a year old, but a large study in the US found that less than 7 per cent of cot death babies had a history of ALTEs. A two-year study in Sweden covered 4 out of every 10 births and found that none of the babies who suffered an ALTE went on to die of cot death.

The chances are that ALTEs have nothing to do with cot death. They may, possibly, indicate that a baby is vulnerable to breathing problems, but they don't provide any meaningful clues to resolving the puzzle of the sudden infant death syndrome which affects so many healthy babies. Some babies have died of 'cot death' whilst in their parents' arms, and some could not be resuscitated even when skilled people were present. That doesn't sound like the apnoea of an ALTE.

Sudden Adult Death

In 1996 there were reports of at least two cases of sudden unexplained death in adults – both healthy girls aged 17 and 18. The victims of what is referred to as sudden cardiac death (SCD) have healthy hearts and no signs of infection or stroke. As with cot death, the post mortem can't pick up any signs that anything is amiss so doctors can only speculate about the cause of death. It's possible, for example, that the chambers of the heart stop beating in sequence, setting up a dangerous rhythm that leads to death. This arrhythmia, as it is called, may be the result of abnormalities in the impulse system which prompts the heart, or it might even be caused by strong emotional excitement – an extreme version of your heart skipping a beat. Could something similar happen in cot death?

What Might Happen in Cot Death?

Without concrete evidence from post mortem examinations it's impossible to tell what happens during cot death. It's very likely that there's no one single answer in any case. There's no shortage of theories – just a lack of facts to prove or disprove them. In addition to the idea of faulty heart rhythms, respiratory failure and inherited metabolic defects, recent suggestions include:

◇ Failure to produce 'heat shock proteins' in response to stressful conditions such as infection or overheating. These proteins are normally produced when the body encounters a stress of this kind and they have a role in protecting against subsequent stressors. Without them, so the theory goes, a baby might be particularly vulnerable.

◇ A faulty immune response leading to the production of 'superoxide'. This in turn stops blood vessels dilating and could starve the heart of oxygen.

◇ Failure to react normally to airway obstructions.

◇ Dreaming about life in the womb. From Perth in Australia comes the theory that cot death may be the result of a baby dreaming about his life (or memory of life) as a fetus. In the course of that dream, since a fetus does not breathe in the usual sense, the baby may stop breathing and die. Although this may sound a little far-fetched, there is laboratory evidence to support the idea that adults process stored memory when they dream and that the sleeping body makes muscle movements to correspond with the dream image. But it's not a theory you could ever prove in relation to newborns.

◇ Poisons produced by bacteria, on their own or in combination with nicotine from cigarette smoke. Researchers at the University of Manchester showed that the toxins produced by bacteria from the noses of cot death victims could kill chick embryos, particularly when they were mixed with very low concentrations of nicotine.

It's likely that new theories will keep emerging. Chapters 10 and 11 outline some of the other theories and the possible risk factors that are currently being investigated.

Key Facts

- Cot death is a mystery that can't be explained in medical terms.

- It's quite normal for babies to stop breathing for a short time – up to 15 or 20 seconds.

- Babies who stop breathing for longer than this but then recover are said to have suffered an 'apparent life threatening event' or ALTE.

- So far there's no evidence of a connection between cot death and ALTEs.

- Most cot death babies seem to die peacefully in their sleep without any pain or suffering

Chapter Three

CAUSES: THEORY AND FACT

Most of us will never meet someone whose baby has died of cot death. Statistically speaking the chances are slim, unless your job brings you into regular contact with young babies and parents. On the other hand you may well hear of a cot death, through a friend of a friend, and it's only natural to wonder and to speculate about the baby and the circumstances of his or her death. After all, who dies of cot death? Are there some special characteristics that make cot death more likely? Or can it really just happen out of the blue?

The stories behind the statistics tell us that cot death isn't the preserve of the rich or the poor. It doesn't respect race, it can happen to apparently perfectly healthy babies and, yes, it can and does happen completely out of the blue.

There is no single answer to cot death. It's possible in some cases that there's one factor which leads to death. In others, and probably in the majority of cases, it's likely that the baby is subjected to a variety of problems at a particularly vulnerable stage in his development and that this combination of factors leads to cot death. Some experts describe it as a 'biphasic' or two-stage event: in the first stage something predisposes the baby to cot death, and in the second stage something happens at a critical time in the baby's development. (Official statistics use the term 'sudden infant death' to include all deaths where there has been any mention of cot death, crib death or SIDS, even if other causes of death are also listed.)

Post mortems play an important part in detecting problems or complications that may have been involved and can be used to eliminate possibilities, while research focusing on the way babies develop in the first six months of life – their breathing, the way their heart rate changes and matures, electrical activity in the brain, nutrition and infection – can highlight the vulnerable times.

Other research (epidemiology) concentrates on details about the baby's life and that of his or her parents – age, gender, social conditions, birthweight, location and so on. By comparing this information with facts about the population as a whole, researchers can produce hypotheses and identify risk factors. Official cot death statistics can also tell us a certain amount about the babies who have died of cot death and therefore the things that seem to make cot death more likely.

Making Sense of Statistics

So, for example, we know that the babies who die of cot death are more likely to be boys than girls, to be aged under six months and to have weighed less than 1500g (about 3lb 5oz) when they were born. They are also more likely to have just one parent, to come from poor working-class backgrounds, to be born outside marriage to a young mother with three or more other children and to die in the winter months.

This kind of information can point researchers in the right direction as they try to sort out pieces of the puzzle. It's less helpful when it comes down to individual families anxious about the possibility that their child might die of a cot death. Baby girls with a higher than average birthweight born to a professional married couple in their early thirties with no other children could still die of cot death in June, July or

August. The statistics tell us is that it's less likely, but it's by no means impossible.

The following paragraphs look in more detail at the statistics. If you're not keen on statistics you might want to skip ahead to page 35.

Age

Cot death is most common in babies under six months old. In the five years from 1991 to 1995, for example, 84 per cent of sudden infant deaths occurred among babies aged under six months. The most vulnerable seem to be between one and three months old. Almost half (49 per cent) of cot deaths in this period were in babies under three months old.

Very few children over a year old die of cot death. In 1995, for example, 398 babies died of cot death compared with only 18 children aged over one year. Official statistics on sudden infant death actually exclude figures for children aged over 12 months.

Risk of Cot Death (England and Wales, 1995 figures)

Baby's Age	Risk
Birth to 1 month	1 in 13,500
1 to 3 months	1 in 3830
3 to 6 months	1 in 4950
6 to 12 months	1 in 12,960
12 to 24 months	1 in 36,000
Overall Risk	
Birth to 12 months	1 in 1630

Gender

Cot death is more common among boys than girls – and has been consistently so for many years, although the gap seems to be narrowing slightly as the number of cot deaths falls. Overall, between 1991 and 1995, about 62 per cent of all cot deaths occurred among boys, although only 51 per cent of all babies born were boys. As with so many things about cot death, the reason for this remains a complete mystery.

Time of Year

Most cot deaths occur in the winter months (see the following graph). At least, that's the pattern that emerges when you look back over the last five years. In the period 1991 to 1995 there were 62 per cent more sudden infant deaths in the three months from January to March than there were in the three months from July to September. In real number terms, for every 10 cot deaths in these summer months, there were around 16 in the winter ones.

On the basis of this, researchers at the University of Aberdeen have calculated that the time of year a baby is born can influence his or her risk of cot death. They found that babies born in February to May have a lower risk of cot death (one third lower) than those born in August to November. A baby born in September has twice the risk of a baby born in April.

But the last five years have seen a dramatic decline in the number of cot deaths and it's possible that the seasonal pattern might be changing. If you look at the figures for 1995 alone there are no great differences between winter and summer – in fact there were 183 deaths in October to March against 215 in April to September. However, it is wrong to make any judgements about what is happening on the basis of one year's statistics. As with so much in cot death research, we have to wait and see.

Sudden Infant Deaths and
Month of Death, 1991–1995

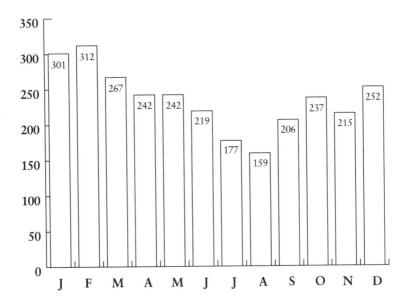

Region

Researchers have investigated the possibility that cot deaths might be more common in some parts of the country, but there's no clear pattern. In 1989 to 1991, the cot death rate in the south west of England was almost double that in the northeast Thames region, but by 1992 it had fallen back to below average for the whole of England and Wales. In 1995 – the latest year for which figures are available – the north west of England had the highest cot death rate (0.97 per 1,000 live births) and northwest Thames the lowest (0.3 per 1,000 live births). With such a rapidly altering picture it seems fairly unlikely that geographical location has anything to do with cot death.

Birthweight

The smaller the baby at birth, the greater the risk of cot death. Babies who weigh less than 1500g (about 3lb 5oz) are ten times more likely to die of cot death than babies who weigh 3500g or more (over 7lb 13oz). But most babies who die of cot death will have a healthy birthweight – over 3000g (6lb 11oz). In 1995, for example, nearly 53 per cent of cot death babies weighed over 3000g at birth. How can that be?

The answer lies in the distinction between death rates and actual numbers of deaths. Because there are so many babies in the 'healthy birthweight' category, even if their overall cot death rate is low, the actual numbers who die of cot death can be high. In 1995 there were 7583 low birthweight babies (under 1500g) and 24 died of cot death. That's a relatively high death rate of 3.16 per 1000. By contrast there were 489,024 babies weighing over 3000g, of whom 208 died of cot death. That's a relatively low death rate of 0.43 per 1000.

Looking at it another way, although three quarters of babies were born weighing more than 3000g, as a group they suffered only half the cot deaths. Whereas the low birthweight group represents just 1.2 per cent of babies, as a group they suffered 6 per cent of cot deaths.

Mother's Age

The younger the mother, the greater the risk of cot death. The statistics show that babies are most at risk of cot death when their mothers are under 20 at the time of delivery. Babies whose mothers are under 20 are almost eight times more likely to die of cot death than babies whose mothers are aged 30 to 34. Mothers aged 40 or more are least likely to have a baby die of cot death. The figures are quite startling (see table overleaf).

Mother under 20	Mother 40 or more
41,926 babies born	11,330 babies born
87 cot deaths	2 cot deaths
death rate of 2.08	death rate of 0.18
per 1000	per 1000

On the other hand, because relatively few young women give birth, nearly four out of five mothers of cot death babies are over 20.

Marital Status

Babies born outside marriage are at greater risk of cot death. In 1995, the cot death rate for the babies of married couples was 0.32 per 1000 live births. Among babies of unmarried parents it was 1.17 per 1000. Even among babies of unmarried parents living together the rate was 0.9 per 1000. The highest cot death rate (1.98 per 1000) was among babies whose births were registered by a single parent.

Other Children in the Family

Couples expecting their first child may take some comfort from the fact that cot deaths are relatively rare among first-born children. The fourth child in a family is over three times more likely to die of cot death than the first.

Social Class

Social class is defined in terms of what the father does according to the information on a baby's birth certificate. Both inside and outside marriage, the lower the social class, the higher the risk of cot death. Inside marriage, the babies of fathers with so-called 'unskilled occupations' (for example, porters and labourers) are more than four times more likely to die of cot death than babies of fathers with professional occupations (doctors, lawyers and so on). Outside marriage the difference is even greater – as much as six times the risk.

Multiple Factors

There's an old adage that you can prove anything with statistics, and when you look at the types of issues which have been investigated in the production of the official cot death statistics you might wonder just what it is researchers have been trying to prove. How can a baby's gender, the age of his mother, the marital status of his parents and the job done by his father have anything to do with the chances of him dying for no apparent reason? Why pick on these aspects of his life?

The answer is that this is the information that can be gleaned from a child's birth and death certificates. On its own, the information isn't that useful but historically it has pointed the way to further areas of investigation. Do more young single mothers smoke, and might smoking put babies at risk? Does the timing of cot deaths mean that temperature is a factor? If people with lower incomes live in poorer housing conditions, are their children more vulnerable to infection and might there be a link between infection and cot death? These are the kinds of questions that researchers have taken up, leading to confirmed risk factors associated with smoking and sleeping position and other possibilities such as oversheating, bottlefeeding and bed sharing. These are explored in Chapters 4 to 9.

As more risk factors become established, and parents take note and change their behaviour, it's possible that these statistical trends will change.

Key Facts

- ◆ Cot death can affect any baby.

- ◆ Babies are more likely to die of cot death if they weigh less than 1500g (about 3lb 5oz) at birth, are boys aged under six months, are born outside marriage to a young mother, are the fourth or fifth child in the family or have a poor working-class background.

- ◆ Eight out of ten cot deaths occur in babies under six months old.

- ◆ After the first month, the risk of cot death decreases as babies get older.

Chapter Four

SLEEPING POSITION

Babies are at greater risk of cot death if they sleep on their tummies. This is now an established fact and new parents are invariably advised to put babies to sleep on their backs.

In fact, until the 1960s very few babies in the UK slept on their fronts. The practice probably began to change in the 1960s and 1970s when premature babies in special care units were laid down this way to help them breathe better and stop them inhaling any vomit. It's perhaps not surprising that the practice extended to healthy babies. After all, every parent wants their baby to breathe well and avoid choking on vomit. But this ignores the fact that these premature babies had special problems that wouldn't apply to healthy full term babies. In fact, there's no evidence that healthy full term babies benefit in the same way from being put to sleep on their tummies.

The idea that sleeping position might have something to do with cot death was put forward in the 1940s. It wasn't until the late 1980s and early 1990s, however, that researchers found widespread evidence to support the idea, and in 1991 campaigns were launched to alert parents. These campaigns have produced quite widespread changes in the way parents put babies to bed, but there are still some parents who have yet to hear about them or act on the advice.

What's the Theory?

In fact no-one has ever produced a satisfactory theory to explain why sleeping on his front puts a baby at greater risk of cot death, but there have been lots of very plausible suggestions:

◇ The lower jaw and tongue could be pressed backwards by the weight of the baby's head on the mattress and so create an obstruction in the airway. Technically this is possible, but it has never been shown that babies sleeping on their front have more or longer pauses in their breathing.

◇ The cartilage of the nose could be deformed by the weight of the baby's head, causing a blockage, or the nose could be blocked by an infection. Again, technically, it is possible that with such a blockage the baby would breathe in faster, creating a drop in pressure which could collapse a particularly vulnerable part of the respiratory tract. It's also true that not all young babies are able to switch to mouth-breathing when their noses are blocked, although this reflex is thought to be established by the age of five or six months (after which age, of course, the risk of cot death is considerably reduced).

◇ Airflow could be obstructed by the mattress or bed coverings. This 'suffocation' theory was discounted about 50 years ago, but it is the belief behind the Hong Kong practice of putting babies to sleep on their backs and it might be an extra factor when babies are found with their heads covered or faces pressed into the mattress.

◇ Extending the head backwards could put pressure on large blood vessels in the neck and reduce the oxygen supply to the brain. This theory dates back to 1979 but seems to have been ruled out by more recent studies using nuclear magnetic resonance scans.

◇ Overheating. Lying on your front reduces heat loss. Along with too much clothing or bedding and a high temperature caused by infection, this could lead to hyperthermia – overheating. This theory is explored in Chapter 6.

◇ Rebreathing expired air which is naturally short of oxygen.

◇ Bacterial toxins. As an adult, lying on your tummy when you've got a cold can increase the production of mucus and encourage bacterial growth and the toxins associated with it. Might these toxins be responsible for the deaths among babies lying on their fronts?

◇ Inhaling toxic gases. This is the theory put forward by those who believe toxic gases can be released from mattresses when they are attacked by fungal growth (see Chapter 9).

◇ Babies who die of cot death and are found face down may have been born with, or may have acquired, a defect in the arousal-head-turning response – the normal response to lack of oxygen. Or they may have been prevented from turning their heads by the weight of bed covers.

Background to the Evidence

The evidence that sleeping on the front is a cot death risk mounted slowly but steadily over a couple of decades. For example:

◇ In 1970 a study in Northern Ireland found that 7 per cent of babies who died of cot death were usually placed on their fronts, compared with 4 per cent of babies who survived. In the same study, 11 per cent of cot death babies were usually placed on their backs compared with 34 per cent of babies who survived.

◇ In 1985 a researcher noted that cot death was rare in Hong Kong where babies were invariably put to sleep on their backs.

◇ Also in 1985, a German study found that 81 per cent of cot death victims were found on their fronts compared with 40 per cent of a matching group of babies who survived.

◇ In 1986 a comparison of cot death rates in different communities found a correlation between high rates and a cultural practice of putting babies to sleep on their fronts. The rate was lowest among South Sea Islanders who place infants on their backs and highest among Maoris whose babies sleep on their fronts.

◇ Australia and New Zealand also published reports in 1986, followed by France in 1987, England in 1988 and the Netherlands in 1989: in each case, more cot death babies were found on their fronts than their backs.

◇ In 1989 a New Zealand study (published in 1991) matched cot death cases with a 'control' group of babies and found that 81 per cent of cot death victims slept on their fronts compared with 49 per cent of controls.

◇ Also in 1989 researchers in Hong Kong found 44 per cent of cot death babies lay on their fronts compared with 7 per cent of controls.

◇ In 1990 a study in Avon likewise found that cot death victims were more likely than controls to sleep on their fronts.

What all these studies showed was that cot death could be linked to sleeping position – they didn't prove the connection. The only way to do that was to intervene – to see what happened when you told a group of people to put their babies to sleep on their backs:

◇ In 1987 there was increasing public awareness of sleeping position in the Netherlands and parents were advised against lying babies on their fronts. The incidence of cot death fell by 40 per cent in a single year.

◇ In Avon, between 1989 and 1991 the percentage of parents putting babies to sleep on their fronts fell from 58 per cent to 28 per cent. Over the same period the cot death rate fell by 51 per cent.

◇ In England and Wales as a whole, the incidence of cot death started to fall in 1989 but the fall accelerated following the *Back to Sleep* campaign which began at the end of 1991. In 1991 there were 1008 cot deaths; in 1992 there were 531. In one evaluation, researchers at Addenbrooke's Hospital in Cambridge found that 21 per cent of mothers put their newborn babies to sleep on their tummies before the campaign compared to just 4 per cent of mothers afterwards. (They were also less likely to use duvets and more likely to share a room up to the age of six months, however, so not all the drop in cot death can be put down to changes in sleeping position. See Chapters 5 and 8 for more details about duvets and room sharing.)

◇ In the third year of a large study in New Zealand, the number of babies put to sleep on their tummies halved and the cot death rate fell by about 25 per cent.

◇ In Tasmania the rate of cot death among a sample of babies thought to be at greater risk fell from 7.6 to 4.1 per 1000 when the percentage sleeping on their tummies fell from nearly 30 per cent to just over 4 per cent. The researchers calculated that about three quarters of the reduction in cot deaths could be put down to the changes in sleeping position.

◇ In Norway before a campaign, 64 per cent of babies slept on their tummies. After the campaign only 8 per cent did so. Over the same period the cot death rate fell from 3.5 to 1.6 per 1000.

Questions and Answers

Q *How big is the risk?*

A It has been calculated that a baby sleeping on his or her front has between three and eight times the risk of cot death as a baby sleeping on his or her back. But not all babies who die of cot death are found lying on their fronts and the great majority of babies who sleep on their fronts don't die of cot death.

Q *Back or side?*

A The weight of evidence suggests that the safest sleeping position for a baby is on his or her back. Under the age of six months only a few babies will turn right over onto their fronts from this position. But if you put babies to sleep on their sides they can roll – usually onto their backs, but sometimes onto their fronts. In one study, 63 per cent of cot death victims had been put to sleep on their fronts, but 81 per cent had been found on their fronts. A very recent study – part of the Confidential Enquiry into Stillbirths and Deaths in Infancy (CESDI) – found that less than 4 per cent of babies in the control group turned from side to front, compared to nearly 40 per cent of babies who died of cot death.

Putting a baby to sleep on his or her side doubles or even trebles the risk of cot death. But side is still better than front. If you find your baby sleeps better on his or her side, you can make the position more stable by getting the lower arm well in front of the body. Using wedges or rolled up sheets behind the baby isn't a good idea – it makes it more likely he or she will roll onto the front.

Q   *What if I find my baby has turned onto his front?*
A   As babies get more mobile you'll find they often move around in their cots, finding the position in which they feel most comfortable. So with the best will in the world, after the age of six months or so, parents aren't going to be able to guarantee their babies will stay sleeping on their backs. You might hear it said or implied that once babies have this kind of mobility there's no need to worry about the risk of them sleeping on their tummies. In fact there's no evidence to support this except the statistics which show how rare cot death becomes after the age of six months. But if you do go in to check your baby in the evening or before you go to bed and you find he is sleeping on his tummy, then turn him over. Keep this up for a while, but don't panic if he keeps turning back onto his tummy – he's obviously more comfortable that way. As Joyce Epstein, Secretary of the Foundation for the Study of Infant Deaths, says: 'It would soon drive the parents mad with anxiety if they felt they had to keep getting up during the night to turn him over, and that wouldn't do anybody any good.'

Although it hasn't been explored in any research, logically there seems to be a good case for saying that once a baby is six months old he is stronger and more able to throw off blankets if he gets too hot or to move into a position where he can breathe more easily.

Q   *What's the risk of inhaling vomit?*
A   There is no evidence that healthy full term babies who sleep on their backs are any more likely to inhale vomit and choke than babies sleeping on their fronts.

Q *Does the advice apply to everyone?*

A The advice to put babies to sleep on their backs applies to all parents except those of a tiny minority of babies including those who have Pierre-Robin syndrome or persistent gastro-oesophageal reflux. If you are told that your baby is at particular risk of airway obstruction, has breathing difficulties or a reflux problem, then you may be advised to put him or her to sleep on the front. It's worth talking through with your doctors the relative risks involved. As a general rule, if you're not told to put your baby to sleep on his front then you should put him to sleep on his back.

Don't panic if your midwife puts your newborn baby to sleep on his or her side. They sometimes do this because it can help to clear mucus secretions in the mouth. Ask your midwife if this is relevant to your baby. In fact there are very few cot deaths among babies less than three weeks old, but unless there are medical reasons for putting your newborn baby to sleep on his or her tummy or side, it's worth starting as you mean to go on: babies can quickly get used to the way they're put to sleep and may resist any changes.

Q *Do babies sleep better on their backs?*

A Unfortunately it seems the answer is no – babies sleep longer and cry less when they sleep on their fronts. One study found that babies not only cried twice as much when they slept on their backs, but they had more nappy rash and self-inflicted scratches than when they slept on their fronts. It's possible that sleeping on the front helps with colic (whatever that really is) since the same study found that half the babies stopped crying when placed on their stomachs whereas babies who cried while lying face down only stopped occasionally when placed on their backs. There is a certain logic in this preference for the tummy-down position, since slight pressure on the abdomen might be comforting. Anecdotal evidence also supports the idea that babies prefer this position. Certainly, many opt for it when they are older.

But this preference also causes problems and is one of the reasons why many parents today find themselves faced with conflicting advice on sleep position from health professionals and the older generation of relatives. Mothers who reared children in the 1960s and 1970s are likely to favour putting babies on their stomachs to sleep and will almost certainly have experience of doing this. This conflict of ideas can produce a lot of unhelpful tension in the early days, especially if you have a colicky baby who can't settle to sleep. You want to stick to the expert's advice but you're told you're making a rod for your own back. Chapter 14 has been written especially for grandparents to help them understand the reasons for the new advice, and you may find it helpful to show this chapter to your mother if you are having trouble standing your ground!

Research in East Anglia showed that the majority of parents do now put babies to sleep on their backs. The report, published in the *British Medical Journal* in 1996, looked at the sleeping arrangements for babies born in 1992 and 1993. In 1993 six out of ten newborn babies were put to sleep on their backs compared to four out of ten in 1992. Only 3 per cent of newborn babies were put to sleep on their fronts in 1993. The researchers also noticed that, except in one case, none of the babies sleeping on their fronts were firstborns in the family. In other words, virtually all first time parents seemed to be acting on the advice about sleeping position.

Key Facts

- Parents can reduce the risks of cot death by putting babies to sleep on their backs. This is the safest sleeping position.

- A baby who is put to sleep on his or her front has a 3 to 8 times increased risk of cot death.

- Lying on the side is more risky than lying on the back, but better than lying on the front.

- A baby who is put to sleep on his or her side has a 2 to 3 times increased risk of cot death.

- Nobody knows why sleeping on the front increases the risk of cot death, although there are lots of theories.

- There is no evidence that healthy full term babies benefit from being put to sleep on their tummies.

- There is no evidence that babies who sleep on their backs are more likely to inhale vomit and choke.

- Some pre-term babies and a very few others may benefit from sleeping on their fronts: doctors will always advise parents when this is necessary.

Chapter Five

OVERHEATING AND ILLNESS

It has been suggested that overwrapping a baby can cause overheating and unexpected death, particularly if the baby is lying on his tummy or has an infection.

What's the Theory?

The human body can tolerate a wide range of temperatures, although there are limits. Prolonged exposure to extreme heat or cold can kill and babies have been known to die in an unheated room on a cold winter's night, or in a locked car parked in the sun. But babies who die of cot death don't show the classic signs of either heatstroke or hypothermia.

At first glance the historical pattern of more cot deaths in the winter months might seem to suggest a stronger link between cot death and hypothermia, but in fact the reverse seems to be true, with overheating as an emerging risk factor. The overheating theory actually fits the figures because in winter parents tend to pile on the blankets and turn up the heating, even on days when the temperature is not particularly low. That the seasonal pattern of cot deaths seems to be disappearing now (see Chapter 3) may be a tribute the education campaigns targeted at parents over the past few years.

Clothing, bedding, room temperature, the weather and all sorts of inherited beliefs and ideas can influence how hot babies are allowed to get, both when they are healthy and when they are ill.

The head has a particularly important job to do in controlling temperature. If a baby is heavily wrapped in a cot, 85 per cent of her total heat loss may be through the head. If the head is covered with a hat or with blankets the baby won't be able to lose enough heat. For several reasons, this is made worse if the baby is lying on her tummy. First, the surface area in contact with the mattress is greater (22 per cent compared to 15 per cent). Secondly, because leg movements are likely to make the blankets rise over the back of the head and the baby won't mind this, whereas lying face up, not only are the blankets more likely to be kicked off by leg movements, but if they were to rise up the baby might well wake up because they would come into contact with the cheeks which are particularly sensitive. And thirdly, the baby is more likely to curl up in the tummy down position and this reduces heat loss further because there is a greater degree of skin to skin contact.

The head is also important because it is a major site of heat production. No-one knows exactly what would happen if the temperature rose inside the brain, but it's known that heat stress can cause apnoea, or pauses in breathing, the baby's equivalent of a convulsion brought on by a fever.

Background

A study published in the *Lancet* in 1984 found that 94 per cent of cot death victims were overwrapped, in an unusually warm environment, hot and sweaty when found dead or ill with an infection which wouldn't normally be expected to cause death.

Another study, published in the *British Medical Journal* in 1990, found that babies who died of cot death in Avon and north Somerset were more heavily wrapped than a parallel group of babies of the same age and from the same communities. A higher proportion of the cot death victims had also been in rooms where the heating was on all night. The research showed that overwrapping a baby increased the risk of cot death whether or not the baby was lying on his tummy. This was confirmed by some research in Australia, published in 1992. The researchers described the babies who had died of cot death as 'significantly overdressed for a given room temperature' and they found the babies' body temperatures were not low even though the readings were usually taken about seven hours after the babies were last seen alive.

The Confidential Enquiry into Stillbirths and Deaths in Infancy found that nearly 22 per cent of babies who died of cot death slept in rooms where the heating was on all night compared to less than 12 per cent of babies in a control group. The babies who died were also more likely to be heavily wrapped, and more of them were found with the covers over their heads.

The overheating theory may also help to explain the different cot death rates in different countries. In New Zealand in the past they have tended to wrap babies up well, place them on their tummies and use soft mattresses or sheepskins which increase the surface area in contact with the baby – and the incidence of cot death has been high. In Hong Kong parents tend to wrap quite heavily but the babies lie on their backs – and the incidence of cot death is low. In Scandinavia babies are put to sleep on their tummies but they are lightly dressed – and the incidence of cot death is low again.

However, most experts agree that overwrapping and high room temperatures on their own are unlikely to cause cot death. It seems that overheating can play a part, but it's more likely to be in combination with infection.

Infections: Is There a Connection?

No-one has been able to make a direct link between a specific infection and cot death. But as a general rule, infections raise metabolic rate and can increase body temperature. They can also affect the airways: most upper respiratory tract infections such as the common cold, tonsillitis, laryngitis, sore throat and croup cause nasal congestion which makes it difficult for babies to breathe through the nose or feed properly; whilst lower respiratory tract infections, such as bronchiolitis, lead to inflammation in the bronchi or breathing tubes. So it doesn't seem unreasonable to think there may be a link of some kind between respiratory infection and cot death. However, the picture is still very fuzzy, despite several serious studies.

For example, there's no real support for the idea of a link from the death certificates of babies who die of cot death. It is possible for doctors to record more than one cause of death on a death certificate. But so far as cot death is concerned, this doesn't happen very often – on only 49 out of 398 occasions in England and Wales in 1995. And respiratory infections or diseases were mentioned only 11 times.

Of course, this on its own doesn't prove or disprove anything and figures from elsewhere suggest that the link with infection may be slightly greater. A series of 95 sudden unexplained deaths among babies in Avon and north Somerset was studied and it was found that infection explained death in three cases and may have contributed to death in a further 37.

Research in Melbourne over a decade ago found that babies who died suddenly over the age of three months were more likely to have signs of infection than a matched group of surviving babies, and an even older study from the UK, published in 1978, showed that major signs of illness were four times more common in babies who died of cot death than in a matching group of babies who survived. But the babies chosen for the matching group were not studied at the same time of year and didn't live in the same areas, so the results weren't conclusive. When these problems with the control group were put right in a subsequent study, the researchers found there were no significant differences between the two groups in terms of the signs of illness reported. However, they did find that nearly 1 in 5 babies who died of cot death had been seen by a doctor in the previous week, compared to just over 1 in 20 babies in the control group. This suggests that for some babies there might be a link between illness and cot death, but there are no specific signs. One research group did suggest that recurrent episodes of sweating might be an indication that a baby was vulnerable to cot death, but this hasn't been backed up with any further research evidence.

The Confidential Enquiry into Stillbirths and Death in Infancy found that having features of illness requiring professional advice is associated with an increased risk of cot death, but three out of four babies who die of cot death have only minor symptoms or signs, or none at all, prior to death. So again, there's no clear and obvious link. New and more sensitive laboratory tests are being developed which may help to isolate signs of infection at the post mortem stage, but even the researchers who are hopeful about this approach concede that it is highly unlikely viral infection on its own is the 'cause' of cot death. Once again, it's the potential combination of factors which may make particular babies vulnerable.

Infection and Overheating

Overall, the weight of evidence suggests that infection on its own does not increase the risk of cot death – so long as babies are lightly wrapped. The combination of heavy wrapping and infection appears to increase the risk of sudden death quite considerably. There is some evidence that when a baby has an infection parents tend to pile on the blankets, probably in the belief that the child needs protecting from the cold or will be comforted by the weight and pressure of the bedding. It seems that nothing could be further from the truth.

Experts have calculated the approximate amount of bedding babies need (see Chapter 12) and this is a useful general guide if, as a parent, you feel uncertain what to do. But the fact is that most healthy babies can tolerate a wide range of temperatures – their bodies can adapt by altering the amount of heat they conserve or lose. When they are ill and their body systems are already in upheaval this may not apply, of course, which would explain why the combination of infection and heavy wrapping seems so significant. Unfortunately, although the advice about overheating was included in the 1991 *Back to Sleep* campaign, it does not seem to have been taken up in the same way as advice about sleeping position. Research in East Anglia showed that in both 1992 and 1993 one in four newborn babies was put to sleep under a duvet – despite all the advice to the contrary. By the time the babies were six months old more than a third were under a duvet.

Key Facts

- ◆ Overheating as a result of high room temperature or too many blankets, or both, may contribute to cot death.

- ◆ The risk is greater when overheating is combined with sleeping on the tummy or an infection.

- ◆ Most babies get ill at some time and there's no evidence that infection or illness on its own causes cot death.

- ◆ There's no evidence that seeing a doctor will prevent cot death, but parents should call a doctor if their baby is ill since the baby may need treatment (see Chapter 12).

Chapter Six

SMOKING

Smoking has now been established as a major risk factor in cot death. In countries where the vast majority of babies now sleep on their backs, smoking may be the single most important preventable risk factor for cot death. In the UK, it has been estimated that the number of cot deaths could be cut by almost two thirds if parents did not smoke. It's true to say that this might be a rather generous estimate, since it's not really known if other factors might come into play once smoking has been taken out of the equation. But in the recent Confidential Enquiry into Stillbirths and Deaths in Infancy, eight out of ten cot death victims came from houses where at least one parent smoked.

Smoking and cot death may be linked in a number of ways – smoking by the mother during pregnancy, smoking by the mother after pregnancy, passive smoking by the mother during pregnancy (if her partner smokes, for example) and passive smoking by the baby. Researchers are still trying to untangle the various strands, but there is no doubt that smoking is linked to cot death. For example, it's now known that smoking during pregnancy and afterwards doubles or even trebles the risk of cot death for the baby, and the risk increases with the number of cigarettes smoked. Even if you feel you are unable to stop smoking there are steps you can take to minimise your baby's exposure to smoke.

What's the Theory?

No-one knows exactly how and why smoking increases the risk of cot death. There are various theories:

◇ Smoking during pregnancy reduces the flow of oxygen and nutrients to the baby and restricts his or her growth. It also increases the risk of premature labour. And both premature and lightweight babies are at greater risk of cot death. But this can't be the whole story since even full term, average birthweight babies are at greater risk of cot death if their mothers smoke.

◇ The hypoxia (lack of oxygen) caused by the carbon monoxide in tobacco smoke might have an effect on the unborn baby's developing respiratory control system. This in turn could make the baby susceptible to early infection and overheating.

◇ A study of 295 babies in Oklahoma showed that those whose mothers had smoked during pregnancy were more likely to suffer from apnoea – times when they stopped breathing.

◇ Smoking in pregnancy could interfere with the developing baby's heart. Animal experiments have shown that nicotine interferes with the release of a chemical which keeps the heart beating properly when there is a lack of oxygen to the brain. It also impairs the ability of the heart to beat faster in response to stimulation by adrenaline.

◇ Passive smoking by babies and young children is known to increase their chances of respiratory infections which may in turn leave them more vulnerable to cot death (see Chapter 5).

◇ In the developing baby, nicotine may be taken up by parts of the brain involved in controlling the heart, arousal, sleep and muscles. It's possible this could affect the brainstem adversely and might therefore leave the baby without the resources to cope with the events that precede a cot death – whatever they may be.

◇ Babies of smokers may have smaller airways and fewer small air ducts in the lungs, making them vulnerable to breathing difficulties and unable to respond in the event of a problem.

None of these theories is proven fact and research is ongoing. It's actually very unlikely that there is a single mechanism linking smoking and cot death, but rather a combination of factors which leaves the baby vulnerable. What's certain is that smoking during pregnancy is not good for babies and that there is a link of some sort with cot death.

The Evidence

The evidence to indict smoking comes from all over the world. A study in the Netherlands, for example, looked in detail at 15 low birthweight or premature babies who died suddenly and unexpectedly. Twelve out of 15 of the mothers had smoked – that's a smoking rate of 80 per cent, compared with 40 per cent among other mothers.

A Finnish study found that 52 per cent of cot death mothers had smoked during pregnancy compared with 21 per cent of other mothers. And in the UK, in Avon, 55 per cent of cot death mothers reported smoking during pregnancy, compared with 33 per cent of other mothers.

In Hong Kong there were only 16 cases of cot death between 1986 and 1987. None of the mothers had smoked (because it is culturally unacceptable) but 50 per cent of the fathers had smoked, compared with 22 per cent of other fathers.

Questions and Answers

Q *How great is the risk?*

A Overall, if parents smoke the risk of cot death for the baby doubles or trebles. Studies in different parts of the world have produced slightly varying results so it's difficult to be precise, but there's widespread agreement that the more the parents smoke, the greater the risk of cot death.

In New Zealand, babies whose mothers smoked during pregnancy had a fourfold increased risk of cot death compared to babies whose mothers did not smoke. Even after adjusting for all the other possible cot death risk factors, smoking still increased the risk by two thirds. In Sweden, smoking up to nine cigarettes a day almost doubled the risk of cot death and smoking ten cigarettes or more per day nearly trebled the risk, compared with non-smokers. In Cardiff, smoking less than 20 cigarettes a day doubled the risk of cot death while smoking more than 20 a day produced a fivefold increase in risk. In Germany, smoking up to 20 cigarettes a day more than doubled the risk while smoking more than 20 a day produced a sevenfold increased risk.

Because these studies rely on people reporting the amount they smoke, the results are always slightly suspect. However, it seems more likely that women whose babies have died will deny their smoking or understate the amount they smoke. If that is true, of course, the figures from these studies would be even worse and the risks even greater.

The risks of cot death for the baby seem to be highest in the first eight weeks. In at least one study, researchers looked at the cot death cases where the mother's smoking was identified as the major risk factor and found that the babies were most likely to die before they were eight weeks old.

Q   *Is it smoking or just low birthweight?*

A   It has been known for many years that women who smoke during pregnancy are very likely to have low birthweight babies. It could be argued that it is this, rather than the smoking itself, which puts the baby at risk of cot death. But several studies have shown that smoking is a risk even if the baby has a good birthweight.

Q   *Is there a risk from fathers smoking?*

A   Yes. A large study in Sheffield was used to calculate the relative risks of cot death in families where one or both adults smoked. Compared to two non-smoking parents, if just the father smoked the baby's risk was increased by about a third. If just the mother smoked in pregnancy, the risk was increased by about two thirds. If both parents smoked, the risk more than trebled.

Several studies have confirmed that passive smoking is a factor. In New Zealand one study showed that the risk of cot death actually increased as the number of smoking adults in the house increased. And in the US, smoking during and after pregnancy trebled the risk of cot death, while just smoking afterwards doubled the risk.

The general hazards of passive smoking are well established, but worth repeating in the context of health risks to babies. Tobacco smoke in the air is one fifth mainstream smoke exhaled by smokers, and about four fifths so-called sidestream smoke. This sidestream smoke comes from the end of cigarettes while they burn between puffs. Sidestream smoke has greater amounts of ammonia, benzene, carbon monoxide, nicotine and various carcinogenic chemicals than mainstream smoke. These are greatly diluted in the air, however, which reinforces the idea that parents who smoke can help by creating a smoke-free zone around their baby.

However, it's thought that babies and young children

are particularly vulnerable to passive smoking as their lungs are developing and susceptible to damage. Recent research showed that smoking around newborn babies can cause coughing and wheezing. In comparison with the children of non-smoking parents, children of smokers are more prone to colds, flu, middle ear infections, pneumonia and bronchitis. Chapter 5 looks at the possible links between viral infection and cot death.

Q *Should smokers breastfeed or not?*

A It's a fact that relatively few smoking women choose to breastfeed their babies. There are various possible reasons for this, such as a grouchy baby and problems producing enough milk – both of which are explained when you look at the interaction between cigarette smoke and breastfeeding. For example, smoking lowers the level of the hormone, prolactin, which controls the amount of milk you produce, it interferes with the milk let-down reflex and it reduces the milk supply. It has also been reported that nicotine gets into breastmilk producing nausea, vomiting, abdominal cramps and diarrhoea in the baby.

But breastfeeding has so many advantages for the baby and there's no convincing evidence that cot death is more likely among breastfed babies of smoking mothers than among bottlefed babies of smoking mothers. A recent US study showed a fairly neutral effect, whilst researchers involved in the large New Zealand cot death study in Auckland found that the babies of smokers who breastfed had a slightly **lower** risk of cot death than the babies of smokers who didn't breastfeed. Although no studies have examined this in depth, it seems sensible to suggest that mothers don't smoke whilst they are actually feeding the baby – whether by bottle or by breast or, indeed, at any time when they are with their babies. This will limit the impact of passive smoking.

Giving Up

Surveys by the Health Education Authority (reported in *Smoking and Pregnancy: A survey of knowledge, attitudes and behaviour*, 1996, by Keith Bolling and Lesley Owen) suggest that around 46 per cent of women smoke in the year before they get pregnant and at least 36 per cent smoke at some time during pregnancy. The evidence suggests that the proportion of women who stop smoking during pregnancy is quite small. Those who do stop tend to do so in the first trimester – the first three months. In 1996, 36 per cent of women were smoking in the first trimester, 31 per cent in the second and 30 per cent in the third. That means that at least one in three babies is regularly exposed to tobacco smoke before he is born.

Smokers are more likely to cut down than give up. In 1996, in addition to the four out of ten pregnant women who gave up some time in the year before they were pregnant, a further four had cut down – leaving only one in five who had made no change. Overall, out of 100 pregnant smokers, 25 will give up as a result of pregnancy, 40 will cut down, 22 will make no changes and 6 will give up but start again before the end of pregnancy.

It's not known how many of the women who give up or cut down on smoking during pregnancy will go back to their normal habits after the baby is born. The Health Education Authority's survey showed that about one in ten pregnant women who had just given up thought that realistically they would start smoking again after giving birth.

In July 1992, the government set a target that one in three women smokers should give up at the start of pregnancy by the year 2000. The target – contained in *The Health of the Nation* White Paper – didn't look unrealistic, since the evidence available at that time suggested that one in four women smokers gave up at some point during pregnancy. But despite a six-year campaign by the Health Education Authority,

Stop Smoking Action Plan

- Set a date to stop and get rid of all your cigarettes the night before.
- Get support by telling everyone what you are doing and asking them not to smoke near you and not to offer you cigarettes.
- Break the link which creates the habit: if coffee and cigarettes go together, drink something else; if you reach for a cigarette when watching the TV, then read a book or go for a walk instead.
- Find something to do with your hands – sewing, knitting or painting your nails.
- Focus on being a non-smoker today and take one day at a time.
- Learn to relax – your local antenatal teacher will be able to give you hints and can teach relaxation techniques.
- Reward yourself by saving the money you would have spent on cigarettes and spending it on treats at the end of each week. Or you could keep a record of the amount you've saved and use the money to buy something special for the baby towards the end of your pregnancy.

the latest figures suggest that the percentage of pregnant women who smoke before they get pregnant has actually increased, as has the percentage who continue to smoke while they are pregnant.

The statistics aren't encouraging – but no-one is suggesting that giving up smoking is easy. Not only is smoking an addiction, but for many women it's a response to stress, their main source of pleasure and the only thing that sees them through from one difficult day to the next. On the other hand, thousands of men and women have succeeded in quitting the habit. If it's a question of motivation, then being pregnant and understanding the very real risks smoking poses for the baby may be an important starting point for a personal commitment to quit.

Unfortunately, according to the Health Education Authority's surveys, the message about the dangers of smoking isn't getting through. In 1996 less than two out of five pregnant smokers thought that smoking was very dangerous to the unborn child. About two out of five believed that smoking made you more likely to have a small baby and two out of three thought it didn't matter if a baby was small at birth because

---

Helping Her to Quit

The Health Authority's surveys suggest that men who nag their pregnant and smoking partners to stop could be doing more harm than good. More than seven out of ten women said advice and suggestions from their partner were unhelpful. So what can partners do?

- Give up at the same time – don't just cut down or stop when you are with her; she'll be able to smell the smoke on you and that won't help at all.
- If you don't smoke, give up something that you really enjoy such as alcohol, chocolate or coffee: that way you'll understand more what she's going through.
- Give positive feedback – tell her how well she's doing.
- Plan rewards or treats for the end of each week she doesn't smoke – a meal out, something nice to wear or just a card saying well done.

59

he or she would still grow. Less than one in three thought there was a link between cot death and parental smoking.

There's no shortage of information, advice and support for smokers who want to quit. Midwives and doctors should be able to help and you can call the smokers' Quitline on 0171 487 3000. But if a woman decides to give up smoking for the sake of her baby, her partner may be the most important source of help. If a couple can give up together they can support and encourage one another. It may also help if you decide to make your home a smoke-free zone. If you tell visitors why you are doing this (because passive smoking will certainly put the baby's health, if not his or her life, at risk) you will probably get their support as well.

Key Facts

- ◆ Smoking in pregnancy and afterwards increases the risk of cot death by two or three times.

- ◆ The more you smoke, the greater the risk of cot death.

- ◆ The risk of cot death is also increased if only the father smokes.

- ◆ The risk increases as more adults in the house smoke.

- ◆ Your baby's health will benefit if you give up smoking before you get pregnant, as soon as you know you are pregnant or at any time during pregnancy, although it's not known whether stopping smoking in the later months of pregnancy will reduce the risk of cot death.

- ◆ Smoking during pregnancy is also associated with miscarriage, low birthweight and pre-term delivery.

Chapter Seven

BREASTFEEDING

Breastfeeding is good for babies. Hundreds of studies have confirmed its benefits alongside the real disadvantages of formula milk. So it's tempting to think that breastfeeding might somehow protect against cot death. After all, it protects against illness through the transfer of maternal antibodies, while formula milk makes the immature kidneys work harder and increases the risk of dehydration in hot weather. What's more, anecdotal evidence suggests that bottlefed babies sleep for longer periods at night whilst breastfed babies have more frequent nocturnal contact. Breastfeeding may also bring mother and baby into closer contact, increasing the bond and conferring some of the perceived advantages of room sharing (see Chapter 8). But more than 30 years of research have failed to establish a definite link between bottlefeeding and cot death.

The Evidence

An analysis in 1995 showed that of 18 major studies, 11 found an increased risk from bottlefeeding and 7 found no effect. Such inconsistency on its own would suggest there's no definite link, but in fact the studies can't really be compared because they each took different factors into account. So, while one study may have made allowances for the effect of the baby's sleeping position – a known cot death risk factor – others didn't. Of the 11 studies which did find a link between bottlefeeding and cot death, only one took account of sleeping position **and** smoking during pregnancy.

This single study, published in New Zealand in 1993, found that a baby who was fully bottlefed when leaving hospital had almost two and a half times the risk of cot death as a breastfed baby, even after making allowances for smoking and sleeping position. Experts in New Zealand have calculated that more than one in five cot deaths can be attributed to the fact that the baby is bottlefed by the time he or she leaves hospital. This belief has led to breastfeeding promotion being included in the national cot death prevention programme and to pressure groups in the UK calling for similar action.

But the UK research doesn't support the link. In January 1995 the results of a comprehensive study of infant feeding and cot death were published in the *British Medical Journal*. The researchers concluded that 'bottle feeding is not a significant independent risk factor for the sudden infant death syndrome'. Although they were able to show a threefold increased risk for bottlefed babies, the risk reduced to insignificant levels once they ruled out sleeping position, smoking by the mother, prematurity and the parents' employment – all factors which are believed to contribute to cot death and which therefore complicate the picture.

The study looked at feeding arrangements for all the babies who died of cot death in the Avon and north Somerset area between November 1987 and April 1989 and between February 1990 and June 1991. Each baby who died was matched with two other babies of the same age from the same health visitor's list. These surviving babies made up the control group. All the parents were asked exactly the same questions about feeding, sleeping position, employment, smoking and so on.

The study showed that on the whole bottlefed babies were more likely to suffer cot death but they were also more likely to have mothers who smoked. There was a trend for the risk of cot death to increase with the amount of bottle-feeding – so, for example, a baby who was fully bottlefed had over twice the risk of a baby who had never been breastfed. But once smoking and the other factors were taken into account the difference was simply not significant in statistical terms.

Data from the national Confidential Enquiry into Stillbirths and Deaths in Infancy confirms this: only 45 per cent of the babies who died had ever been breastfed compared to 60 per cent of the babies in the control group, but once socio-economic status (known to be linked to bottlefeeding) was taken into account the apparently protective effect of breast-feeding all but disappeared.

Evidence from Hong Kong also suggests that if there is a link between feeding practices and cot death then it is a weak one: babies are rarely breastfed there but Hong Kong has one of the lowest cot death rates in the world.

The Avon team put forward the idea that there might be other social or cultural factors which lead to bottlefeeding and which, if included in the New Zealand study, would have weakened the apparent link between bottlefeeding and cot death. The majority of mothers in New Zealand breastfeed and it's possible there might be something about those that don't that leaves their babies more at risk of cot death. But the team didn't completely rule out a link, admitting that: 'Larger studies may be able to distinguish a small independent effect of being bottle fed.' The researchers also put forward the idea that bottlefeeding might be part of a chain of events leading to cot death.

Feeding and Smoking

Although smoking is not very common amongst women who breastfeed, it does happen. The results of studies examining the interaction of smoking and breastfeeding are mixed. On the one hand, a team of researchers in California reported that the effects of passive smoking wiped out the protective effect of breastfeeding that they had observed in their study. On the other hand, a team from Auckland, New Zealand, found that the protective effect persisted and the babies of smokers who breastfed had a slightly lower risk of cot death than the babies of smokers who bottlefed. Since experts in the UK aren't convinced that breastfeeding can protect against cot death, the arguments are slightly academic!

But even if the link between bottlefeeding and cot death isn't established, women who smoke and wish to breastfeed have to face some unpleasant facts. For example, smoking lowers the level of prolactin – the hormone which controls the amount of milk you produce; it interferes with the milk let-down reflex; and it reduces the milk supply. Nicotine can also get into breastmilk producing nausea, vomiting, abdominal cramps and diarrhoea in the baby. At the very least, women who smoke should not do so while they are breastfeeding, in order to limit the effects of passive smoking on the baby.

Key Facts

- ◆ There is no clear evidence that breastfeeding protects against cot death.

- ◆ Babies who are bottlefed are more likely to have mothers who smoke, to have been premature and to come from poorer families. These are the factors which are linked with cot death.

◆ Taking account of smoking in pregnancy, prematurity and unemployment reduces the apparent link between bottlefeeding and cot death so it is no longer significant in statistical terms.

◆ Being fully bottlefed is not a significant independent risk factor for cot death.

◆ Breastfeeding has real health advantages for babies. Compared to babies fully breastfed for three or four months, bottlefed babies are five times more likely to be admitted to hospital with diarrhoea, twice as likely to be admitted to hospital with respiratory infections, twice as likely to suffer middle ear infections, five times more likely to develop a urinary tract infection, twice as likely to develop eczema or a wheeze if there is a family history of allergy and twice as likely to develop diabetes as a child.

◆ More than a third of women do not give their babies any breast milk at all and only four out of ten women are breastfeeding at six weeks after birth.

Chapter Eight

ROOM SHARING AND BED SHARING

Babies are less likely to die of cot death if they share a room with their parents. That's the conclusion of a recent study in New Zealand. The researchers investigated the sleeping arrangements of nearly 400 babies who died of cot death in the years 1987 to 1990 and nearly 1600 matched babies who made up the control group. The babies with the lowest risk of cot death were those who shared a bedroom with an adult and slept on their backs. The study also had something to say about relative risks of different sleeping positions and arrangements. Among the babies who slept on their backs, those who slept in a separate room had more than double the risk of those who shared with their parents. On the other hand, among the babies who shared a room with their parents, those who slept on their fronts had three times the risk of those who slept on their backs. It's the combination of back sleeping and room sharing which seems so powerful. Interestingly, room sharing with other children did not affect the risk of cot death either way.

The researchers didn't speculate why babies should benefit in this way from adult company but it's a haunting thought that babies could be more likely to die when they are on their own. Is it really possible that they get lonely? Could the noise of adults breathing stimulate their own breathing in some way? Or are parents are able to react more intuitively to their child's needs when they are close?

Putting babies to sleep on their own is a relatively recent development in western societies and isn't common to all communities. For example, a report published in 1989 showed that room sharing was the norm in the UK Bangladeshi community – where the incidence of cot death was very low. And in the frequently crowded living conditions in Hong Kong, room sharing is inevitable – and the cot death rate is very low.

Experts in the UK haven't made any specific recommendations about room sharing yet – the evidence really isn't strong enough at this stage. And, to be fair, the New Zealand research group did say further studies confirming the findings were needed before any public health recommendations were made. But in a recent update on cot death for doctors, Dr Shireen Chantler, secretary of the Scientific Advisory Committee at the Foundation for the Study of Infant Deaths wrote that: 'There are benefits in encouraging parents to keep the baby's cot in their bedroom for the first 6 months of life', although it's impossible to say yet if the benefits include a reduction in cot death risk. The six-month period relates to the fact that cot death is rare in babies over the age of six months (there's a risk of about 1 in 13,000 for babies aged six to twelve months).

Room sharing hasn't been advocated widely in the UK and really isn't that popular beyond a few months. Research in East Anglia found that nearly nine out of ten newborn babies share a room with their parents. Over half are still there at the age of three months, but only a third by the time they are six months old. This is probably due in large part to the baby's sleeping habits: by the time they are six months old most babies don't need to be fed at night.

But if babies do benefit from adult company at night, would they benefit from sharing the same bed? The answer seems to be no.

Bed Sharing

On the face of it, there seem to be many advantages to sharing your bed with your baby. Anecdotal evidence suggests it helps with bonding, enables new mothers to get more sleep and prolongs breastfeeding with all the advantages that offers. And so far as cot death is concerned, it seems logical to assume that being so near your baby you'd be in the best position to detect any changes in breathing pattern and act accordingly. It has even been suggested that the adult breathing pattern or just the stimulation of having someone close by can help to stabilise a baby's erratic breathing. Advocates of bed sharing point to the low cot death rate in Hong Kong and among the Bangladeshi community in the UK where babies may not only share their parents' room, but also share their bed.

But the limited research evidence available at the moment appears to point the other way. Far from protecting against cot death, bed sharing in certain circumstances seems to increase the risk.

What's the Theory?

First, it's possible that bed sharing is a bit of a red herring, since many parents take a baby into bed with them when he or she is unwell or restless and it could be this illness rather than the bed sharing which predisposes the baby to cot death (see Chapter 5). Alternatively, it has been suggested that the baby could get too hot in the parents' bed or be at risk of 'over-laying', particularly if the parents have been drinking alcohol or taking drugs.

Another idea is that babies sharing a bed might end up rebreathing expired air which is naturally short of oxygen. Ask any mother who has ever shared a bed with her baby and she'll confirm the findings of the study which showed that babies sharing their parents' bed tend to put their faces within a few inches of their mother's. In theory, prolonged breathing in of expired air could lead to hypoxia.

The Evidence

Unfortunately, as with so much of the research into cot death, the evidence isn't clear cut – at least not yet. Further research and larger studies will help to build up a more comprehensive picture. Meanwhile, there are contradictory findings about the interaction of bed sharing with smoking and alcohol.

Research in New Zealand some years ago found that bed sharing increased the risk of cot death, particularly if the mother smoked. Drinking alcohol didn't seem to be involved, it made no difference if the baby had been restless or not and an increased temperature in the bed wasn't relevant. There was also no evidence that overlaying was involved – if it was, all babies would be at equal risk, whether their mothers smoked or not.

A more recent New Zealand study confirmed the risk for both smokers and non-smokers, but again put the emphasis on smokers who bed share. The report suggested that while 26 per cent of cot deaths were explained by bed sharing among smoking mothers, only 3 per cent could be explained by bed sharing among non-smoking mothers.

In the UK, however, while there is some research confirming the risk of bed sharing if the mother smokes, researchers didn't find an increased risk for the babies of non-smoking mothers. In contrast, they did find that alcohol was involved and came to the conclusion that bed sharing increases the risk of cot death if the mother has recently been drinking alcohol.

The strong connection of cot death and smoking doesn't mean that bed sharing is a red herring in this context. Bed sharing definitely seems to have an effect of its own for babies whose mothers smoke: among these babies, those who share the bed as well have a higher risk of cot death.

Some of the statistics suggest that the effect of bed sharing – whatever it is – can build up over time. So the more time the baby spends in the parents' bed, the greater the risk. In the New Zealand research, babies of non-smoking mothers only had a notably increased risk of dying of cot death if they regularly spent more than five hours a night in their mother's bed. This cumulative effect might explain the rather strange finding that the cot deaths among bed sharers don't necessarily happen while the baby is in the parents' bed.

This finding, and the fact that the risk seems to stay the same whether there are one or two adults in the bed with the baby, seems to rule out any connection with overlaying and overheating since these would be much more likely if there were two adults in the bed.

The theory that there might be a connection with breathing expired air fits the pattern of greatest or even exclusive risk for the babies of smokers. For if all babies are at some risk from breathing expired air when they sleep with a parent then the risks must surely be greater for babies who are breathing expired air containing tobacco components. This would also tie in with the finding that the effect of bed sharing appears to be cumulative – the damage wrought by what is in effect passive smoking would accumulate over time.

But there's no concrete proof. The research on bed sharing is at an early stage and it appears to be a very complex issue. It is difficult to explain some of the statistics which have emerged – the New Zealand finding that the babies of non-smoking mothers are more at risk if they have bed shared at some time in the last two weeks than if they bed shared in the last sleep, is a good example. And not all studies support the idea of a connection: for example, a Californian study reported in the *British Medical Journal* in 1995 found no significant link between routine bed sharing and cot death.

More research is needed to sort out these apparent anomalies, to establish conclusively whether non-smoking parents put their baby at risk if they bed share and to define more clearly the mechanism by which bed sharing could pose a threat.

In the meantime, what should parents do? Research in East Anglia suggests that although six out of ten newborn babies share a bed with their parents on occasion, only one in ten does so regularly. Nevertheless, expert advice in the UK is not to bed share – take the baby to bed with you by all means, especially if it helps with breastfeeding, but always return the baby to his or her own cot to sleep (see Chapter 12). A good compromise might be a Bed-Side-Bed cot which hooks on to the side of your bed. Call 0181 989 8683 for more details.

Key Facts

- ◆ The risk of cot death may be lower if your baby shares your room – but not your bed – for the first six months.

- ◆ The risk of cot death appears to increase if the baby shares a bed with his parents and his mother is a smoker.

- ◆ Babies whose mothers already smoke have an increased risk of cot death. This risk is increased even further if the baby shares a bed with his mother.

- ◆ Mothers who are finding it hard to stop smoking can help their babies by avoiding bed sharing.

- ◆ The risk of bed sharing to the babies of non-smoking mothers hasn't been clearly established.

Chapter Nine

MATTRESSES

There is no concrete proof that chemicals used in the manufacture of cot mattresses have anything to do with cot death. But since the question was raised several years ago, it seems it just won't go away. That's hardly surprising, though, since few parents could be philosophical when faced with the idea that they might be putting their babies to sleep in a cloud of toxic gases. The mattress theory also appeals because it would give us something to blame, something tangible although mysterious, scientific and outside our control (since we as parents don't manufacture mattresses). But the evidence which has emerged so far is contradictory and incomplete and the majority of cot death experts in the UK and elsewhere are still to be convinced there is a connection.

What's the Theory?

The theory is that substances used as plasticisers and fire retardants in the manufacture of PVC (polyvinyl chloride) mattress covers, or in the mattresses themselves, could break down as a result of fungal growth and release highly toxic gases which might then cause cot death.

It's an appealing and plausible theory because it does seem

72

to tie in with some of the known risk factors and statistics for cot death. For example:

◇ Babies sleeping face down would be at greater risk since the toxic gases, being heavier than air, would settle around their faces.
◇ Subsequent babies would be at greater risk than first-borns since they are more likely to have an old mattress which is more likely to be harbouring fungal activity.
◇ Babies born to unemployed parents and single mothers would be more likely to have second-hand mattresses.

But Does the Theory Fit With the Facts?

So far, experts say no. Or rather no, but . . . , since the government committee which overturned the original 'evidence' also recommended that there should be investigations into the potential toxicity of additives used in cot furnishings and that the levels of arsenic in the fire retardant in question – antimony – should be as low as possible. What's more, the committee members said there should be further research on microbial infestation of cot mattresses and covers since they did find there were more active fungi growing in mattresses used by babies who died of cot death than in other mattresses.

Background to the Theory

So far as the UK is concerned, the theory originated with Mr Barry Richardson, a consulting scientist with his own laboratory. He specialised in the deterioration of materials and became interested in cot mattresses and cot death as a result of a chance conversation in 1988 about fungal damage to PVC.

Initially Mr Richardson was looking for evidence that

arsenic reportedly used in PVC cot mattress covers could release the highly toxic arsine gas if it was attacked by a fungus called *Scopulariopsis brevicaulis*. The fact that arsenic can degenerate in this way is well established. In fact, it's the stuff of murder mysteries: in the nineteenth century, arsenic-pigmented wallpaper would release the fatal gas when attacked by fungus. But nobody had made the connection with cot mattress covers. (In fact, arsenic is rarely used in cot mattresses, although trace amounts may be present as impurities in the fire retardant antimony which was commonly used at the time.) When Mr Richardson grew *S. brevicaulis* on some cot mattresses samples he was unable to generate arsine and unable to find any arsenic. What he thought he'd found instead were phosphine and stibine – toxic gases produced from the breakdown of phosphorus (used as a plasticiser) and antimony (used as a fire retardant).

He then tested mattresses used by babies who'd died of cot death and reported finding *S. brevicaulis* in all of them. He also believed that each mattress had generated at least one of the toxic gases: arsine, phosphine or stibine. That was June 1989.

The issue became a scientific controversy when independent studies organised by the investigating government committee (the Turner Committee) and the Foundation for the Study of Infant Deaths couldn't substantiate or confirm Mr Richardson's findings. In fact, in some respects they challenged his scientific methods and cast doubts on his test results. That was in 1991.

In 1994, the story bubbled up again as a result of a Cook Report shown on television. The programme presented the results of new tests which seemed to confirm a risk from antimony, but these were quickly followed with studies which refuted the 'evidence', and a QED programme from the BBC which did something of a demolition job on the whole theory.

With the balance of 'evidence' swinging from one camp to

the other it's not surprising that many parents have either panicked or been left totally bewildered about what to do for the best. And it's doubtful whether busy health visitors, midwives and doctors could have kept abreast of the developments to such an extent that they would have felt confident giving advice to parents.

The saga seemed to end with the findings of the Confidential Enquiry into Stillbirths and Deaths in Infancy that:

◇ Babies using second-hand mattresses were not more likely to die of cot death.
◇ Using a mattress with an integral PVC cover was associated with a significantly lower risk of cot death than using any other type of mattress.

But these findings have themselves been disputed by those who genuinely believe cot mattresses are the key to cot death and further studies have been commissioned. Meanwhile proponents of the theory are convinced they have made the vital breakthrough in cot death research and even assert there has been a deliberate cover-up.

The disputes centre around complex chemical and biochemical laboratory tests. So complex, that highly qualified and experienced technicians cannot agree about methodology and reporting. So what have they found?

Laboratory Findings

What Mr Richardson and subsequent researchers did was to grow some of the organisms colonising the mattress and then use silver- or mercury-based papers to detect gases being produced. Mr Richardson believed he had found *S. brevicaulis* on all the mattresses he tested and used test papers to show that some gas or gases were being given off.

But there's some doubt whether the colour changes on the test papers were specific to phosphine or stibine and the indicator papers couldn't provide information about the quantity of gas produced. In fact, people argued, all the colour changes could show was that a gas of some kind was being produced. Repeat tests at the Laboratory of the Government Chemist, the International Mycological Institute at Kew and Birkbeck College at London University found the colour changes occurred randomly and didn't identify a particular gas. Later tests suggested that the changes were due to sulphur given off as the micro-organisms were cultured. But in this instance, it was argued, the test papers might have been contaminated to start with. More detailed tests in 1995 appeared to show that the colour changes occurred because of bacterial growth – whether or not there was any mattress material present – and were not due to phosphorous, arsenic or to antimony. The Turner Report summarised:

'*We accept that Mr Richardson observed colour changes in indicator papers during his experiments. However, we have not received sufficient quantitative or detailed qualitative data to convince us there are no alternative interpretations of the effects he observed, particularly as we consider the indicator tests used to be equivocal and not specific to the gases "identified" by Mr Richardson.*'

Researchers also disagreed that *S. brevicaulis* was the main organism on the mattresses, although the International Mycological Institute did find it in 3 out of 19 cot death mattresses and 1 out of 31 controls. The Turner Committee also expressed doubts about the way Mr Richardson had stored the mattresses, suggesting that contamination could have occurred during storage. What's more, it's unclear whether the infestation had been correctly identified as *S. brevicaulis*. There was a suggestion that Mr Richardson had misidentified a harmless bacteria as the fungus, a bacteria which is part of the *Bacillus* species which is commonly found in the home. (To a lay person this may seem incredible, but the disagreement centres around the notion that the fungus *S. brevicaulis* could appear in two different forms, one of which might closely resemble a bacteria.)

Micro-organisms **can** lead to the deterioration of plastics. That's a fact. And arsenic, itself toxic, **can** be transformed to the toxic gas arsine under laboratory conditions. But there's very little arsenic in cot furnishings. And according to the expert Turner Report, it's very unlikely that the phosphate plasticiser used in PVC would break down under attack from micro-organisms. The experts on the Committee also thought it would be very difficult for phosphates to convert to phosphine. Likewise, they couldn't find any evidence that antimony was consistently broken down by microbes to produce toxic gas. The Turner Report says:

'Laboratory studies using sensitive and specific methods could not detect such gases, even when using "spiked" samples of mattress material, i.e. samples to which relatively high concentrations of soluble antimony and phosphorus compounds were deliberately added to provide ideal conditions to obtain gas formation.'

The Committee concluded that there was no evidence relating to antimony or phosphate-based additives but it did agree that if any toxic compounds could be produced from cot furnishings then they were most likely to come from compounds used as additives – in other words, fillers, plasticisers and fire retardants. The Committee recommended that manufacturers give careful consideration to the need for these chemicals, their potential toxicity and the likelihood that they would be broken down.

Post Mortem Evidence

In 1990, Dr Neil Ward of the Trace Element Unit at Surrey University found higher than normal levels of antimony in the blood of some babies who died of cot death. The levels ranged from 0.002 to 0.005ppm (parts per million), up to five times the normal 0.0009ppm. But adults can have up to 0.06ppm of antimony in the blood and not suffer any ill effects, so these results on their own don't prove anything, certainly not that antimony was the cause of death. Besides which, the study was tiny: a much larger study would be needed before any conclusions could be drawn.

In fact, levels of antimony have been tested in several other studies, with conflicting results. A 1994 study found antimony in the livers of 22 out of 40 babies who died of cot death compared with only 1 out of 15 babies dying of other causes. But a 1995 study found the average amount of antimony in 25 babies dying of cot death was less than that among 25 babies dying of other causes. And research published in 1995 showed that (in this respect at least) it made no difference whether babies dying of cot death had slept on PVC mattresses or not – levels of antimony were the same.

The human body has no need of antimony, so it is a pollutant. But it is found in the general population and there's a possibility that babies might be exposed to it whilst in the womb, since it has been detected in foetuses. Babies can also have antimony in them within 24 hours of birth when they've had hardly any exposure to mattresses.

Exposure to arsine, phosphorus and stibine would normally produce a range of symptoms including nausea, vomiting, headache and shortness of breath. It would also produce changes in the red blood cells which should be picked up during a post mortem. The Turner Committee concluded that either there has been no toxic gas poisoning among cot death cases or babies are sensitive to very low levels which don't affect the cells. There is also a characteristic garlic smell following exposure to the gases and there are no reports of this from post mortems following cot death.

Storm in a Teacup?

To say that the whole question of mattress safety has been a storm in a teacup is to belittle the investigation, the serious nature of cot death and the fact that testing continues in an attempt to provide a definitive answer, one way or the other. The mattress saga started with a serious scientific investigation into a very reasonable and valid hypothesis but degenerated into scientific controversy, media hype, confusion and hysteria. The mattress theory of cot death still has its advocates but the general feeling at the moment among the doctors, paediatric pathologists and epidemiologists specialising in cot death is that there is no convincing evidence and no need for parents to do more than ensure their baby has a dry, clean and firm mattress to sleep on (see below). But we await the results of further investigations.

The best news for parents would be if all cot mattress manufacturers could guarantee that their products were free of all antimony and phosphorous compounds – and several have taken action. Mothercare, for example, stopped using antimony back in 1991 and many other retailers and manufacturers have followed suit. But the current British Standard allows both antimony and arsenic, up to a specified maximum level (1982 British Standard for Domestic Bedding BS 1877 Part 10 – the specification for mattresses and bumpers for children's cots).

Many mattresses may now have reduced levels of phosphorus but this is much harder to achieve since phosphorus compounds are used in so many things. There is no maximum level prescribed in the standard.

The best advice for parents expecting their first child is to buy a new mattress if you can afford it, check with the retailer and manufacturer (if necessary) that it does not contain antimony and then keep it clean and dry. For parents who want to re-use a mattress for a second or subsequent baby, the best advice is to store it carefully – completely enclosed in wrapping. If you are at all worried about the possibility of fungal contamination and the release of toxic gases from a second-hand mattress or one you have already bought, you can first of all check with the mattress manufacturer to see if antimony and phosphorous were used and secondly, wrap the mattress in polythene. This is a precaution based on logic rather than experiment: nobody knows if it will make a difference, just as nobody knows for certain whether there is or isn't a link between cot mattresses and cot death.

When the Experts Disagree . . .

The controversy over testing methods and the interpretation of results isn't helpful to anxious parents; nor is the suggestion that vested interests are at work in hiding the truth. In summary the two sides disagree over the following points.

- Whether cot deaths occurred before the introduction of PVC and foam-based cot furnishings.
- Whether the fungus *S. brevicaulis* grows routinely in cot mattresses.
- Whether you can consistently generate arsine, stibine and phosphine gases from infected mattresses.
- The methodology for testing which gases have been generated.

Soft Mattresses

Perhaps because PVC coverings haven't been widely used on cot mattresses in New Zealand, some research there has focused on the type of mattress – firm versus soft. In a large study researchers found that soft cot mattresses more than doubled the risk of cot death. This was nothing to do with the babies' sleeping positions – in other words, a soft mattress didn't make it more likely they would sleep face down. In fact, it's not clear why it should be relevant unless it contributes to overheating. But the conclusion was that parents should avoid buying or using soft cot mattresses. This research confirmed a UK finding from way back in 1965 that soft mattresses were a risk factor for cot death.

Key Facts

◆ Most experts on cot death say that PVC covered mattresses are not linked to cot death.

◆ Best advice is to keep your cot mattress clean and dry. If you need to store a mattress once it has been used (between babies, for example), make sure it is completely enclosed, stored in a dry place and well aired before it is used again.

◆ Use a firm mattress.

◆ Replace a mattress if it shows any signs of deterioration.

◆ Babies don't need pillows, so don't use them.

Chapter Ten

OTHER THEORIES AND POSSIBLE RISKS

The mystery of cot death has been an open invitation to the theorists. Some of the resulting hypotheses about possible causes and risk factors may seem slightly odd – ranging from a rapid second stage in labour through routine immunisations and on to the use of nappy sterilisers. But when the stakes are so high researchers can't afford to ignore suggestions. It's vital to check out possibilities in case another piece of the jigsaw can be fitted. Even when a theory is tested and found untenable, progress is made and parents can gain some comfort and encouragement.

This chapter outlines some of these 'alternative theories' and the evidence to support or negate them, along with some of the other established associations.

Alcohol

Alcohol consumption in pregnancy is not linked to cot death but drinking alcohol may increase the risk posed by bed sharing (see Chapter 8). However, the findings are contradictory and there is no concrete evidence either way as yet. Pregnant women are advised not to drink excessive amounts of alcohol during pregnancy because of the risk of fetal alcohol syndrome, which is nothing to do with cot death.

Dummies

The Confidential Enquiry into Stillbirths and Deaths in Infancy found that babies who died were no more or less likely than other babies to use a dummy, but those who did use one were less likely to use it on the night they died. In other words, there's some evidence that using a dummy may offer some protection against cot death. Researchers in New Zealand came to the same conclusion when they analysed their figures. But both sets of experts are very cautious about interpreting the data this way and don't go so far as to recommend dummies for cot death prevention. Using a dummy could be nothing more than a sign that the mother follows a particular pattern of baby care which is protective, although it has been suggested that the dummy might play a part in preventing the tongue falling back and blocking the airway.

In the past, parents and childcare experts have sometimes discouraged the use of dummies for a variety of reasons including:

- The risk of teeth being pushed out of position. In fact, research suggests that any effects are small and disappear when the dummy sucking habit is broken. The risks are greater for children who suck their fingers, so dummies might be recommended for them.
- The risk of dental caries. But this is only a problem if the dummy is sweetened.
- The possibility that dummy sucking may get in the way of successful breastfeeding.
- Difficulties breaking the habit as the child gets older.
- The baby or child being unable to get back to sleep at night if the dummy falls out.

But there is no evidence whatsoever that using a dummy increases the risk of cot death.

Ethnicity

In the UK, Asian babies seem to have a considerably lower risk of cot death – about half that of the white population. This ties in with a very low rate of cot death in Hong Kong where, it is suggested, there may be some as yet unidentified cultural factors which protect babies.

Family History of Cot Death

Many studies suggest that babies born to parents who have already suffered a cot death do have a slightly increased risk of dying suddenly and unexpectedly. Estimates from outside the UK vary as to just how great the risk is – from no increased risk up to 1 in 100 for a single previous death in the family or 1 in 10 if there have been two or more cot deaths among siblings. (The risk for the general population in the UK is about 1 in 1670.) The Foundation for the Study of Infant Deaths says that out of every 500 subsequent babies at least 495 will survive. However, the estimates of risk are so wildly varying that it is difficult to make sense of them. What's more, the studies were done some time ago and we don't know how they relate to the babies dying of cot death in the latter half of the 1990s. Nevertheless, it's possible that a few cot deaths – probably less than 1 in 100 – are due to inherited disorders such as an enzyme deficiency.

If someone you know has suffered a cot death and is concerned about the risk to future children, individual advice and reassurance is vital. The Foundation for the Study of Infant Deaths has devised a special programme – the CONI programme – for parents who have suffered a cot death and go on to have further children (see Chapter 13).

Immunisation

Some people have suggested that the routine diphtheria, tetanus, polio and whooping cough vaccines given to young babies might be implicated in cot death in some way. After all, the vaccines are given during those early months when babies seem to be more at risk. The possibility was tested recently in two studies. In France, researchers found that vaccinations did not increase the risk of cot death, although when they looked just at the babies under three months old they did find that more of the cot death victims had been immunised than the babies in the control group. However, the French team felt that another study would be needed to confirm whether this was anything like a real risk. In New Zealand, babies who didn't have their six week, three month and five month vaccinations were twice as likely to die of cot death as babies who had all their immunisations. In this case, researchers concluded that far from increasing the risk of cot death, immunisation might actually lower it. This is similar to UK findings but there has been no recent research here.

Intra-uterine Growth Retardation (IUGR)

Analysing the statistics has established that very low birth-weight babies are at greatest risk of cot death (see Chapter 3). Babies can be tiny because they are born too soon or because they do not grow normally during pregnancy – or a combination of the two. There's some research to suggest that this failure to grow in the womb – called intra-uterine growth retardation (IUGR) – may be more significant than being premature so far as cot death is concerned. The theory works along the lines that a baby who hasn't received the right nutrients or the right quantities of nutrients at critical stages of his or her development may have certain organs or body systems which haven't developed normally and which may be more vulnerable to outside influences such as infection or overheating. It's not that the organs are abnormal; it may simply be that they aren't so robust and don't have any spare capacity for dealing with emergencies. Research in Liverpool has shown that growth retarded babies could have fewer filter units in their kidneys. These filters are essential for removing waste from the body and have extra work to do when the body is fighting an infection. A similar situation could occur in the lungs where growth retarded babies may not have the full complement of ducts which transport oxygen to the blood. So the ducts they do have work harder and the lungs can be put under strain. It's not hard to see how a combination of IUGR and passive smoking could raise the risks of cot death.

IUGR can be caused by poor diet or smoking during pregnancy, by an infection or by the very high blood pressure seen in pre-eclampsia. Further research is examining the development of the placenta which is the baby's sole source of food in the womb.

IUGR isn't only a factor for small babies: babies with an apparently normal birthweight and no visible signs of any problems can be growth retarded – they simply should have been heavier. On the positive side, it's thought that many of the problems of IUGR disappear after six months.

Nappy Sterilisers

It has been suggested that the chemicals used to clean nappies might cause cot death. The idea was tested in the large New Zealand cot death study which involved the parents of nearly 400 cot death victims. Their nappy cleaning practices were compared with those of nearly 16 other sets of parents. The researchers found very little difference between the two groups: soaking nappies in sterilising solution and then rinsing them in water wasn't any more risky than other nappy cleaning methods.

Rapid Second Stage of Labour

Pushing for less than 16 minutes in the second stage of labour doubles the risk of cot death, according to the analysis of some figures in the New Zealand cot death study. Researchers were trying to work out whether things that happened ante-natally or during labour could have any influence on a baby's risk. They didn't suggest any reason why a short second stage should be a problem, although generally it's recognised that the baby's head has less chance to mould during a rapid second stage and many people believe this can lead to problems later such as persistent crying. Whether there is a link with cot death is another matter. (There could be a simple explanation for the apparent link – for example, the increased crying could encourage parents to opt for the tummy down sleeping position which some babies seem to find more comfortable.) The New Zealand researchers concluded that any increase in cot death risk arising from obstetric events is slight in comparison with that from the major risk factors such as smoking and sleeping on the tummy.

Short Pregnancy Interval

In Oregon in the US, women who got pregnant again less than six months after their babies died of cot death tended to give birth to lighter babies than those women who waited more than six months. But the average birthweight was still nearly 3000g (6lb 11oz) which means they were still at relatively low risk of cot death.

Twins, Triplets and More

This is a fairly well established risk factor. In the large New Zealand cot death study, twins, triplets or other multiples had three times the risk of cot death as singleton babies. Even so, the risks are still small. Multiple pregnancy is not something the vast majority of parents want to influence (despite the fact that selective abortion is now a technical possibility), so this finding is only useful in so far as it alerts parents expecting multiples to the need to follow expert advice on preventing cot death. The same is true for the knowledge that premature, low birthweight babies are at greater risk (see Chapter 3). If a woman goes into premature labour there's nothing she can do to stop it, except follow medical advice. But she and her partner can take steps afterwards to provide the safest possible environment for their small baby. If one baby from a set of twins or triplets dies of cot death, the remaining baby or babies are usually taken into hospital for observation.

Chapter Eleven

WHERE NEXT?

Some people think the problem of cot death has been solved. If you've read the preceding chapters then you'll know that it hasn't. The discovery of important links with sleeping position and smoking has made the 1990s a decade of great progress, but the work doesn't stop there.

Every year the Confidential Enquiry into Stillbirths and Death in Infancy (CESDI) takes a detailed look at a large number of babies who have died suddenly and compares them with an even larger number of healthy, surviving babies. In the first two years of the enquiry, health visitors interviewed parents of 195 babies who died of cot death and of 780 babies who survived. Each questionnaire covered 600 items including sleeping position, heating, smoking, recent illnesses, bed sharing, room sharing, dummy use, breastfeeding, mattress type (plus age and re-use), use of alcohol and illegal substances, the length of time the baby was left unattended, apparent life threatening events, depression in the mother, previous deaths in the family and recent major life events.

Health professionals reviewing questionnaires for CESDI came to the conclusion that cot death could probably have been avoided in 21 per cent of cases if those responsible for the baby had acted differently, and that there had been less than ideal care that might possibly have contributed to the death in a further 43 per cent of cases. These are hard messages for

89

parents who may be consumed with guilt after the death of their baby and it's important to remember that they are the result of a potentially subjective analysis of the data. But the fact is, even this harsh calculation reveals that in over one in three cases there was absolutely nothing a parent could have done to prevent the death.

So far as CESDI is concerned, it seems the greatest reductions in the number of cot deaths will come from initiatives promoting the key prevention messages to parents whose babies are most at risk – in other words, to smokers and people from disadvantaged backgrounds.

Surveys show that many parents still aren't aware of the basic measures they can take to prevent cot death. In March 1992, very soon after the launch of the *Back to Sleep* campaign, a survey of nearly 800 women found that although nearly nine out of ten were aware of the advice on sleeping position, only half were aware of the connection with overheating and less than two out of ten knew that smoking was a risk. When the survey was repeated in November of the same year, only six out of ten women aged 16 to 24 were aware of the advice on sleeping position.

Detailed research into the possible causes of cot death and the risk factors associated with it continues all over the world and in a wide variety of forms. In the UK alone, researchers are looking into possible links between postnatal depression and cot death, the levels of antimony and other heavy metals in household dust, the association between SIDS and intra-uterine growth retardation (IUGR), the effect of smoking in pregnancy on the baby's respiratory function and the issue of toxic gas release from cot mattresses.

Every year there will be new discoveries, many of them too small to hit the headlines or make dramatic differences to childcare practice, but nevertheless small pieces that fit into the jigsaw and help us see a clearer picture of what lies behind the mystery of cot death. It's fair to say we've probably had the big breakthroughs in the establishment of sleeping position and smoking as major risk factors. But following this incremental approach of detailed and thorough research, it's possible that within the next decade we could have answers to the questions that are still posed by overheating, bed sharing, breastfeeding, infection and household pollutants. And maybe, one day, the problem of cot death will be solved.

Chapter Twelve

PREVENTING COT DEATH

There is nothing you can do as parents to guarantee your baby won't suffer a cot death. But there are lots of things you can do that will reduce the risk.

Parents' safety checklist

- Place your baby on his or her back to sleep.
- Place your baby to sleep in the 'feet to foot' position (see diagram).
- Don't smoke and don't let anyone smoke in the same room as your baby.
- Don't let your baby get too hot.
- Keep your baby's head uncovered indoors.
- If you think your baby is unwell, call your doctor.

It may also help if you:
- Breastfeed your baby.
- Let your baby sleep in your room – but not in your bed – for the first six months.
- Use a new mattress or at least make sure your baby's mattress is firm, clean and dry.

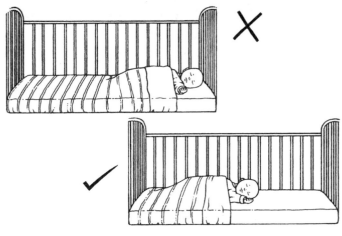

'Feet to foot' guide

The third annual report of the Confidential Enquiry into Stillbirths and Death in Infancy concluded that:

'. . . *current advice appears correct, but is either not being received or not being implemented by a proportion of the population at risk . . . Although there will always be rare but distressing exceptions, it is likely that a further fall in the rate of SIDS would be achieved if ALL parents or child carers were able to adhere to the Key Health Messages.'*

These Key Health Messages are:

♦ **BACK TO SLEEP**
Babies should be put down to sleep lying on their backs, unless there is a substantial medical reason not to do so. Sleeping on the back is preferable to sleeping on the side and sleeping on the front should be avoided.

♦ **FEET TO FOOT – HEAD UNCOVERED**
Babies should sleep in such a way that their head does not become covered during sleep. This is most easily achieved

by putting a baby to sleep with his or her feet close to or touching the foot of the cot. Blankets are preferred to duvets and should be tucked in so that the baby's head is exposed and uncovered without a hat.

◆ NOT TOO HOT
Although it is important to prevent a baby becoming cold, becoming too hot is also a danger. Room heating is not required at night except when the weather is very cold. Babies' bedrooms should be at a temperature overnight which is comfortable for a lightly clothed adult (usually 16–20°C, 61–68°F).

◆ SMOKE-FREE ZONE
Cigarette smoking in pregnancy and around babies increases the risk of cot death. Although giving up would be the best option, a baby will be partly protected if his or her sleeping place is regarded as a smoke-free zone, whether the baby is actually asleep there or not.

◆ PROMPT MEDICAL ADVICE
The risk of cot death may be reduced by seeking prompt medical advice for babies who become unwell, particularly those with a raised temperature, breathing difficulties and who are less responsive than usual. A proportion may have acute infections amenable to treatment.

◆ BED SHARING FOR COMFORT, NOT SLEEP
While it is likely to be beneficial for parents to take their baby into bed with them to feed or comfort, it is preferable to place the baby back in a cot to sleep. This is especially important if the parents smoke or have consumed alcohol.

(taken from CESDI Annual Report, 1994)

Thermometers and Bedding

On its own, it's unlikely that being too hot causes cot death (see Chapter 5). However, studies have found that babies who die of cot death tend to have more bedding or to wear more clothing at night than other babies. This extra heat puts them at an increased risk when they also have an infection or also sleep on their front.

In general, if your baby is sweating or if her tummy feels hot to touch, you need to remove some bedding – particularly if she is unwell or feverish. It's quite normal for hands and feet to feel cool. While you are indoors there is no need to worry about keeping the baby's head warm in cold weather. In fact, babies lose excess heat from their heads so it's very important that the head is uncovered indoors. If you come in from the cold and your baby is asleep, remove any extra clothes or blankets as well. If your baby is feverish she probably needs fewer blankets, not more.

Babies can also overheat because the room is too hot. All night heating is rarely necessary and a baby's room doesn't need to be any hotter than your own. If you're concerned the temperature will drop dramatically in the night you could use a portable radiator or other heater with a thermostat – but don't position it right next to the cot. A temperature of 18°C (65°F) is about right and you can monitor this with a nursery thermometer – very cheap and widely available from Mothercare and pharmacies. You can also buy one from the Foundation for the Study of Infant Deaths. A good nursery thermometer is a starting point for helping you to judge how much bedding your baby needs. The following list is a **very general** guide and assumes that your baby is wearing a vest and babygro.

◇ At 15°C (60°F) use sheet plus 4 layers of blankets.
◇ At 18°C (65°F) use sheet plus 3 layers of blankets.

◇ At 21°C (70°F) use sheet plus 1–2 layers of blankets.
◇ At 24°C (75°F) use sheet only.
   (A blanket folded in two counts as two layers.)

Blankets are the ideal form of bedding since you can easily add and remove them without disturbing your baby. Duvets, quilts, baby nests and sheepskins are not recommended since they can cause overheating and babies should never sleep with a hot water bottle or electric blanket, or next to a radiator, heater or fire.

These specific temperature and blanket recommendations were published by the Foundation for the Study of Infant Deaths (FSID) several years ago. It's possible that you might see slightly different recommendations published elsewhere, but the fact is that it's impossible to be so precise: different babies generate different amounts of heat. The important thing is to feel your own baby (at the back of the neck or on the tummy) to see if he or she is sweating – the recommendations above are just a starting point. This is the message in the FSID's latest leaflet which no longer includes specific temperature and blanket guidelines. The important thing is to keep checking your baby and be prepared to add or take away blankets as required, remembering that it's not just the temperature of the room which counts.

Baby Monitors

Using an ordinary baby monitor may give you some reassurance that you will hear the slightest cry from your baby while he or she is sleeping upstairs or across the landing from you. But there's no evidence that babies dying of cot death cry out. Some reports from parents whose babies died during the day suggest that they do not make any sound whatsoever, they just seem to slip away.

There are other types of baby monitor that can detect breathing movements and, more importantly, when breathing movements stop. These are usually called apnoea monitors (see Chapter 2 for more details about apnoea and apparent life threatening events or ALTEs). There are three main types of apnoea monitor:

◇ A pressure pad or mattress is put under the baby. The pad, which can be battery- or mains-operated, detects changes in the distribution of the baby's weight caused by breathing movements.

◇ A sensor pad is either taped to the baby's stomach or incorporated into an elastic belt which can be put on over the baby's clothes. The pad is connected to a battery-operated electronic device which detects changes in pressure caused by movement.

◇ Two electrodes are stuck to the baby's chest and a mains-operated electronic monitor picks up a small electrical current and any changes caused by breathing movements.

In each case, the monitor rings an alarm or flashes a light when regular breathing movements stop for a certain length of time, usually 20 seconds. Just picking up the baby might be enough to restart breathing, although sometimes you might need to use mouth-to-mouth resuscitation (see page 102) and sometimes it won't be possible to revive the baby.

If parents have already suffered a cot death or if their baby has shown signs of apnoea in the form of an apparent life threatening event (ALTE), then one of these monitors can provide invaluable reassurance. Although there is no proven link between ALTEs and cot death, several studies have shown that babies born to couples who have already lost a child to cot death have a slightly increased risk of losing another. Using a monitor might make it possible for these couples to sleep at night, knowing they have done everything they can to keep their baby safe and well.

But these monitors do have very real disadvantages. For a start, they can give false alarms when the sensor pad becomes detached or breathing movements are very slight. And they won't pick up the kind of apnoea caused by an obstruction in the windpipe. That's because breathing movements continue although there's very little oxygen reaching the baby's lungs. Any kind of twitching may be enough to convince the monitor everything is normal, even if breathing has stopped.

It's also possible to become over-reliant on a monitor, to forget to observe your own baby for signs of illness and to stop trusting your own instincts. It's a bit like giving birth in hospital: it's easy for everyone to watch the high-tech fetal monitoring machine and ignore the woman who is actually experiencing the contractions.

There's no evidence that apnoea monitors prevent cot death. Babies can die while monitors are being used and even if a baby is resuscitated following an apnoea attack, there's no guarantee that he or she would have died if the parents hadn't been alerted by the monitor.

Even so, the British Paediatric Association Respiratory Group suggests that monitors might be used after a baby has had an ALTE and by parents who have already suffered a cot death. In 1993 it was estimated that possibly more than 34 babies were being monitored at any one time in the UK. When monitors are used, it should be under the supervision of a paediatrician or other doctor and the parents should be trained in resuscitation. Monitors are available under the CONI (Care of the Next Infant) programme, directed by the Foundation for the Study of Infant Deaths, or from paediatricians. See pages 122–3 for more details about the CONI programme and the experiences of parents who have used an apnoea monitor for a subsequent child.

Calling the Doctor

It's a real dilemma. On the one hand your baby is snuffly, seems restless and can't settle. On the other hand, it's gone 8pm, the surgery is closed and you're reluctant to call out your doctor for what might be no more than a cold. Patients' concern about 'bothering' the doctor is legendary. It's not just a matter of not wanting to be a nuisance, there's also an issue about looking silly and being labelled as a neurotic mother or over-protective parent. From the doctor's point of view, babies often have minor illnesses and he or she doesn't want to be called out for nothing. But most doctors will say they'd rather make a visit than risk missing something serious and on the whole they do not question the need to visit young babies. The increasingly widespread use of call-out agencies or doctor co-operatives means that it may not be your own doctor you're 'bothering' but someone who has volunteered to work this shift and be paid properly for it. So when should you get help?

When to Call the Doctor

You should call the doctor for advice if your baby has any of the following symptoms which can sometimes develop into a serious illness:

- Highpitched, weak or unusual crying.
- Floppiness.
- High fever and sweating.
- Hoarse cough and noisy breathing.
- Refusing feeds repeatedly.
- Vomiting repeatedly.
- Vomiting green fluid or passing blood.
- Vomiting and diarrhoea.

But you should also call the doctor whenever you think your baby is ill and you are worried – even if he or she doesn't have any of the symptoms listed on page 99. A baby can't tell you what's wrong, but as parents you are in the best position to judge whether something is different about your child. Newborn babies change rapidly but as a rule of thumb, if you haven't encountered this behaviour before and you are concerned your baby might be ill, then call the doctor. If there are no specific symptoms and it's during the day you could call the health visitor first for advice, although she's likely to suggest you call the doctor anyway.

Emergency Action

Reading what to do in an emergency situation isn't really enough, although it's obviously better than nothing and it's good to have a permanent written record of what to do. But nothing can take the place of instruction and practice on dummies. St John Ambulance has a half-day Babies and Children Lifesaver course which is ideal for parents (see Chapter 15).

Dialling 999

You should dial 999 and ask for an ambulance if your baby:

- Stops breathing or goes blue.
- Can't be woken.
- Has a fit or convulsion.
- Has great difficulty breathing or is grunting with each breath.

A card (called a Green Card) summarising advice on when to call a doctor and what to do in an emergency is available from The Foundation for the Study of Infant Deaths. A scoring system to help parents quantify serious illness in babies up to six months old is also available. This system, *Baby Check*, is based on seven symptoms and twelve signs, each of which has a score. The individual scores are added together to give an overall score which will suggest to parents whether they need to see a doctor. *Baby Check* is available to the public (see Chapter 15 for details).

All this is important advice and good training for parents but unfortunately, research has shown that there are no specific signs and symptoms that can alert parents or doctors that a baby might die of cot death. Even so, occasionally what appears to be a cot death may turn out to be the result of an overwhelming infection or a treatable malformation. So it is important that parents get medical advice and help if a baby is unwell.

What Should a Doctor Do?

You've rung the doctor and he or she has agreed to visit or has asked you to take your baby to the surgery. What can you expect the doctor to do? Ideally the doctor should first examine the baby undressed – looking at the colour of the skin, checking for signs of a rash. Then he or she should check pulse, rectal temperature and breathing rate and pattern before giving you advice. Even if there is no need for you to do anything at this stage, you should be told to reassess your baby's condition over the next few hours and invited to contact the doctor again if anything changes. He or she might also suggest you move the baby's cot next to your bed that night so that you are sleeping in the same room. You

Emergency Action

If your baby is not breathing
- Pick the baby up, pinch her gently and flick the soles of her feet to try to stimulate breathing.
- If there's no response, place the baby face up on a table or another firm surface:

    (a) tilt the head backwards and lift the chin to open the airway;

    (b) look, listen and feel for signs of breathing;

    (c) check for a pulse on the upper arm or neck.

If there's no breathing and no pulse
- Start mouth-to-mouth resuscitation by sealing the nose and mouth with your own mouth:

    (a) breathe gently into the nose and mouth five times;

    (b) stop and press five times on the middle of the chest between the two nipples using two fingers (chest compressions);

    (c) breathe into the baby's nose and mouth once;

    (d) for one minute, keep repeating five chest compressions followed by one breath and then take the baby with you while you ring for an ambulance if no-one has done so already;

    (e) repeat the chest compressions and breaths until the ambulance arrives.

If there is a pulse but your baby is not breathing
- Continue the mouth-to-mouth ventilation at a rate of one breath every three seconds.

can ask for advice about the baby's temperature, the ideal temperature of the room and the amount of clothing or bedding required.

It's impossible for doctors to say a particular baby is at risk of cot death on the basis of a physical examination. However, if you are concerned that the doctor has not conducted a thorough examination you could ask to see one of the other doctors in the practice.

Key Facts

- There's nothing you can do to guarantee your baby won't die of cot death.

- There are lots of things you can do to reduce the risk of cot death: follow the safety checklist on page 92.

- A nursery thermometer can be a useful starting point in ensuring your baby doesn't get too hot, but it's the temperature of the baby, not the room, which really counts. There's no substitute for checking your baby, particularly when he or she is unwell.

- Breathing monitors may offer reassurance to parents who have already suffered a cot death but there's no evidence that they prevent cot death and they should only be used in consultation with a doctor.

- Don't be afraid or embarrassed to call the doctor if you are worried your child may be ill.

- Going on a lifesaving skills course can give you confidence to deal with an emergency situation.

Chapter Thirteen

A COT DEATH IN THE FAMILY

Baby Sean

Kerry Gray's son Sean died on 24 December 1982 when he was just one week old. 'I had two kids already, both boys', explains Kerry. 'They'd both been awkward pregnancies with near miscarriages but with Sean everything had been perfect. It was a perfect pregnancy. I felt well and giving birth was like shelling peas . . . completely painless. He was born one week early and he was a perfect baby. He never cried, I had to wake him for his feeds, he fed well and he was great. It was exactly one week later that I fed him about 2 o'clock in the morning. He normally woke about 6 o'clock but that morning it was 7.25 when I went into his room to wake him and he was dead. I think I knew but I tried to warm him up and it was three quarters of an hour before I acted. I ran outside. I was living in a little village and I didn't have a phone. I saw this car coming and I just shouted 'I think my baby's dead'. Someone phoned the doctor and he took one look at Sean and said 'yeah he's dead'. It's nothing like it is now but back then I'd never even heard of cot death. The house was surrounded by police and no-one was allowed out. We were all searched. I was just holding onto Sean and I really didn't want them to take him. It was more painful than you can ever imagine. When the coroner's officer turned up they tricked me into another room and then took him. I was totally hysterical. Then because it was Christmas it wasn't until the first week in January that I heard what he'd died of.'

Baby Sam

Sam Ross died in May 1991 when he was four months old and on the day his mother Di went back to work. 'I left him at the childminder's at about 8 o'clock,' explains Di. 'At 10.15 I rang to see he was okay and all I got was someone crying "the ambulance is coming, he's stopped breathing". Then I was shouting "you've got it all wrong, this is Sam's mum". I was completely hysterical. I phoned my husband and a colleague took me to the hospital and I was there at about 10.45 but we did not see him until 4.30. The childminder's daughter had given him mouth-to-mouth until the ambulance arrived and they'd managed to revive him and he was in intensive care by midday. So we had hope for a while. But when we saw him a machine was breathing for him. He gave out just after midnight when his heart went erratic. It's not a "normal" cot death, but the post mortem report said nothing abnormal was detected and the death certificate says SIDS. He never slept during the day when I had him but the childminder had fed him at 9.30 and then put him down to sleep. She said she kept checking him but I kept thinking "what if I hadn't had to go back to work? Did I miss something? Had he got something wrong that I didn't see?" I don't actually blame the childminder but I've never spoken to her since that day and I can't bring myself to go anywhere near the road where she lives.'

Toddler Daniel

Daniel Bradshaw died of cot death in November 1990 when he was 13 months old. 'He was a fairly light sleeper and tended to wake once in the night,' explains Daniel's father Phil. 'That night he woke around 2.30. I went into his room, gave him a cuddle and a bit of drink and then set him back down. In the morning we assumed he was lying in so we got our elder son up and had showers. Then Jane went in to wake him up and I heard her scream. I ran in and he was cold, lying on his stomach. I took him, laid him on the floor and tried to revive him while Jane phoned the ambulance. We'd no idea how long he'd been dead so I concentrated purely on trying to revive him. We were hoping and praying when the ambulance got here that they could do something. I kept trying until they took him to hospital where he was pronounced dead. But I already knew that. They were very good at the hospital. They wrapped him in a shawl and we could have had as long as we wanted with him.'

Baby Lucy

Lucy Harding died one night in October 1990 when she was eight months old. 'I went to get her in the morning perhaps 20 minutes later than usual,' explains Andrea, Lucy's mother, 'and as soon as I saw her I was pretty sure she was dead. My husband tried to resuscitate her and we called an ambulance which took her to hospital. My husband went with her but I had to stay with my five-year-old daughter. I knew she was dead but it was a total shock. I was completely numb. You think it's not really happening although you know it is. An hour or so later a friend took me down to the hospital and I was able to hold her. We weren't under any time pressure, we were just left alone with her and there was no pressure to give her up which was good.'

Sequence of Events

When a baby dies suddenly and unexpectedly several people have to be involved. To start with the baby's death has to be certified by a doctor. This could be the family doctor, if the parents call one to the house, or a hospital doctor, if they call an ambulance or take the baby to a casualty (A&E) unit themselves. If the cause of death is unknown – as it is in SIDS – the doctor has to inform the coroner (procurator fiscal in Scotland). The coroner sends an officer – possibly a uniformed policeman – to get information from the parents, arranges for the baby to be taken to a mortuary by a funeral director and asks a pathologist to do a post mortem.

The police (CID) usually visit the home routinely if the parents have dialled 999.

If the pathologist can find a cause of death then the parents can register the death. If no cause is found then the coroner may decide to hold a public inquest, after which he or she will write to the registrar stating the cause of death. The baby's funeral can normally take place after the post mortem.

Bereavement

Any bereavement is bound to be painful. But people involved in counselling and supporting the families of cot death victims say that in many cases because of their age, these parents are facing death for the first time. They have no experience of grieving and are totally unprepared for the range and depth of the emotions confronting them.

They may feel empty or numb, angry, afraid, desperate, bewildered and frustrated. Some will cry endlessly, while others will be so stunned that they spend the first few weeks after the death on autopilot. Some will become preoccupied with the dead baby and be unable to talk about anything else, while others will buzz around almost hyperactively, as if keeping busy to avoid thinking about the baby and what has happened. Different people will have different reactions, but it's widely recognised that the majority of bereaved people will go through various stages on the road to accepting what has happened. These stages can include numbness and disbelief; emotional release, anger and guilt; defeat, depression and apathy; and finally acceptance and recovery. Even so, grief can come in waves and there are times when bereaved parents seem to be going backwards rather than forwards.

'I didn't cope at all. I just managed from day to day. There was no support group for bereaved parents at that time and all I had was this woman who met me in the park and said it was good I was young enough to have another one. That was the last thing I wanted to hear.'

'I wanted to lash out and scream and run away. My husband reacted quite differently and he helped a lot as I just sat and cried. My family came down to stay which also helped because even though it didn't happen there, I found I couldn't go back to sleep in the flat unless there were lots of people there. I felt so alone and needed lots of people around me.'

'I felt numb and angry that no-one could tell me why he'd died. He was never ill. He was a healthy little lad. I was so frustrated that something had happened over which we had no control. There was no reason for it. I felt as if something had been ripped away from me and that I was all knotted up inside.'

'It was quite strange really, it was almost us comforting other people because we were quite numb.'

Parents may experience physical as well as emotional reactions to the death of their baby. These can include choking, feeling sick, an upset tummy, extreme tiredness and lethargy, visions of the baby, hearing the baby cry, aching arms, nightmares, inability to concentrate, chest or stomach pain, depression and fear of forgetting what the baby was like. They may even fear recovering, as though 'getting over it' would imply they are callous or were uncaring, unloving parents. These are all very normal reactions.

'For a long time I didn't want to let go. I felt if I let go I was betraying her in some respect. But I read in a book that in letting go you find they're still there; they'll always be with you. A friend said to me that it was as if now I had a "Lucy-shaped" hole in my heart and I think this is an apt description. You never forget them and that love I had for her will never disappear. It will always be with me. The love between a parent and child is always there even if they are no longer physically with you.'

Some parents feel a strong urge to get away from the situation and the places that are causing so much pain. In her book *Cot Deaths: coping with sudden infant death syndrome*, Jacquelynn Luben describes how she and her husband called in at a travel agent's on the day they went to see their dead daughter's body at the mortuary. They just felt the need to escape.

But as the baby's death becomes a reality, parents can and do recover. That's not the same as saying they 'get over it'. They will never get over it. But they start to live again themselves, to take an interest in other things.

'Do I still think about him? Oh God, yes, all the time.'

'To me it's part of my life. If anyone asks me how many kids I've got I say two – one is five and I lost the other one. If that upsets them, then tough.'

'I think in the end, gradually, habit takes over. Things like cooking meals, shopping – it all has to be done.'

'I can't honestly say I think about him every day. But he was toddling around by the time he died so we have so many memories of him. We have pictures up of the two boys together and we've never taken them down. And we planted a memorial tree in the village with a plaque on it and we go to that three or four times a year. Then someone will say "Do you remember when the boys were doing this or that?" My attitude is, he's still part of our lives. We don't make a point of talking about it, but if it comes up in conversation it's not a problem. I don't find it painful. In fact the other day I was watching Luke who's now 11 playing football and one of the mothers watching asked if he was my only child, so I told this complete stranger about Daniel. I've got the attitude that if people ask they'll get the answer. I've got nothing to hide.'

'To an extent the frustration is still there. Even years on, no-one is any closer to knowing why it happens.'

'Not many days go by I don't think of her, but it changes a lot. In the beginning it's very intense – deep feelings which overwhelm you. But thinking now you just remember. She'll always be part of us, integrated in our lives. But it's not overwhelming our lives as it did once.'

'I've probably not come as far as I think and the grieving is still going on. I find it impossible to watch films with sloppy endings. Anything emotional and I end up in tears. Well that never happened before.'

People Who Can Help

- Doctor.
- Health visitor.
- Paediatrician at the hospital.
- Priest or minister.
- Other parents who have suffered a cot death.
- Bereavement counsellors.

The Cot Death Helpline (0171 235 1721) is open 24 hours a day, every day of the year, for bereaved families and those helping them. Staff on the helpline will be able to put you in touch with befrienders or 'Friends of the Foundation' – other parents who have suffered a cot death.

'Lucy was the only one I had images of – for example, I'd pictured her being a bridesmaid for her elder sister. That didn't happen with Kimberley and Rachael and it's still a nagging thought none of that will ever happen.'

'Through the Foundation we were able to meet other couples who had experienced a cot death. It was most odd to get an invitation to visit a couple one evening and find him reading, her doing the ironing and their subsequent newborn asleep in the carrycot on the table. It showed that despite the intensity of a cot death life does return to some normal state in time.'

'I had an excellent health visitor and she was fantastic. She listened and just reassured us we'd done all we could as parents.'

'In the early days we were greatly helped and received a lot of support from FSID. I think we were one of the first people to use their 24-hour helpline.'

Things that may help in the first few days:

◇ Seeing and holding the baby: parents can do this even after the post mortem, in the hospital chapel or in their own home before the funeral. Some parents may want to bathe and dress their baby in some special clothes before the funeral, or they can ask hospital staff to do this.

◇ Memories: some parents may find it helpful to have some final memory of their baby – a lock of hair, a hand print or a foot print. The hospital staff or funeral director can arrange this.

◇ A special service: this could be at the parents' own home or at a place of worship, with special music, hymns and readings led by friends and family. Some parents have a service of thanksgiving some time after the funeral.

◇ Photographs: parents might like to have some pictures of the baby. A member of staff at the hospital may well offer to take some pictures of the parents holding the baby.

◇ Taking the baby to the funeral: it is possible to have the baby at the parents' house before the funeral and the parents could also take the coffin to the church or cemetery themselves.

◇ Ashes: these could be placed in the garden of remembrance at the crematorium or buried in the churchyard.

◇ Book of remembrance: the baby's name can be written in a book of remembrance at church or in the crematorium. Some parents prefer to plant a shrub or small tree in memory of their baby.

Parents are often still stunned by what has happened by the time the funeral takes place. They may find it very hard to cope with all the decisions they are asked to make. As a close friend or relative, you might be able to help by talking through some of these options and offering to help organise things like photographs, flowers and memorials, and by helping them to begin the process of building memories, which they need to do.

'Steve and I insisted we arrange the funeral ourselves and we both felt strongly about that. But I know other people would rather let someone else do it.'

'Some people might think it's morbid, but I took photos of Sam at the chapel of rest. I've only looked at them a couple of times because the memory is still crisp in my mind now. But I'm glad I took them. What if in 15 years my memory of him isn't so clear? You can't turn the clock back then and wish you'd taken them.'

'I kept his bottle and his shawl and the pom pom balls my niece had made him. I've also got my album and a framed picture on the wall. I'd taken a whole film of him the day before he died. I saved all his clothes as well and it was a suitcase that went with me wherever I went. But I eventually gave them to a friend. Sometimes you've got to let go.'

'We've learnt since we could have washed her and dressed her which would have been nice. But you're not in a state to think about things like that when you're so numb.'

'Because she was older we had a lot of pictures of her and people knew her as a little person and we could talk about her as a person. In some ways that helps but in some ways it's harder.'

What Can Friends and Acquaintances Do to Help?

With our great British reserve, many of us are so afraid of doing or saying the wrong thing that in painful situations like these we end up saying and doing nothing. It's easy to persuade yourself there's nothing you can do to help and it's probably true that in the early days very little if anything will comfort grieving parents. But attitudes are important. Parents who have suffered a cot death often speak about people crossing the road or avoiding eye contact and how hurtful this can be. It's also important to remember that bereaved parents need on-going support – they have to face their bereavement every day and it's not something they can forget about after a few weeks. During the weeks and months after the funeral, grieving parents and grandparents may have an overwhelming need to talk about the baby who has died – what they don't need is someone who tries to stop them talking. So don't try to change the subject. As a friend you think it will upset them to talk about their dead baby, but it will upset them more if they are not allowed to do so.

'The most important thing is to be there. But to be honest visitors couldn't win with me. Sometimes I'd want them there and other times I'd think "Why don't they just go away?". And sometimes I found the sympathy a bit too much. I think you get very selfish. You don't think your mother's lost a grandchild or your sister's lost a nephew. You only think about yourself.'

'My mates were there for me. If I wanted to talk about him to my friends there was no problem and that helped a lot. It meant I didn't need to bottle things up.'

'The support of good understanding friends who really just

need to be there, to listen without really having to say much, makes such a difference.'

The boxes below contain lists of DOs and DON'Ts for helping bereaved parents. The questions and answers at the end of the chapter may also help as they address specific situations.

Helping Bereaved Parents: DOs

DO

- Be open in showing your concern and caring: a few words, a gentle touch, even to sit in silence – just being there with them can be comforting.

- Be available – to listen, to help with the children, pets, shopping, the cooking, the ironing, the garden.

- Say you are sorry about what happened to their child and encourage them to talk about her or him as often as they want.

- Allow them to express as much grief as they are willing to share – this may include misery, depression, anger and guilt.

- Talk about the special qualities of their child.

- Reassure them that they did everything they could and tell them of everything true and positive about the care given to their child.

- Give extra attention to brothers and sisters; they too are hurt and confused, possibly frightened and in need of attention which their parents may not be able to give at this time.

DON'T

- Avoid them because you are uncomfortable; being avoided by friends adds pain to an already intolerably painful experience.

- Say 'I know how you feel' (unless you too have lost a child).

- Tell them what they 'should' feel or 'ought' to do. There is no timetable for grieving; each person has to do it at their own pace.

- Change the subject when they mention their child.

- Avoid mentioning the child's name because you are scared of 'reminding' them – they won't have forgotten.

- Try to find something positive about the death (for example, closer ties with the rest of the family or some kind of moral lesson).

- Suggest that they can have another child (it could not replace the child who has died).

- Say 'It's good you've still got other children' – they are not interchangeable.

- Make any comment which suggests that the care given their child at home, in hospital or wherever, was inadequate; parents are riddled with feelings of guilt and doubt without any emphasis from others.

- Let your own sense of helplessness keep you from reaching out to a bereaved parent.

Produced by The Compassionate Friends, a group of parents who've lost a child and who offer support to other bereaved parents (see Chapter 15)

Not Just a Grieving Mother: the Ripple Effects of Cot Death

Fathers Too

It's easy for the grieving mother to become the focus of attention, with the father expected to be strong, to make all the decisions and to return to work within a matter of weeks as though nothing had happened to disturb his routine. This obviously isn't right. As fathers who've suffered a cot death point out: 'He was my son too' or 'I loved her too you know.'

'I feel it was possibly more of a shock for me than for my wife. Cot death probably comes up as a topic of conversation for women but it's not something us men have the opportunity to discuss. The main problem was losing control. There's the old thing about the man being protective towards his family and then this happens and you lose control of the situation. And because of the nature of the death other people take charge and there are lots of things you can't do. There was this real feeling of helplessness because nobody can give you an answer – not the doctors, not the clergy, no-one – and you're trying to piece things together.'

'I can't say my needs as a father were ignored immediately after the event – we were treated the same. But within weeks afterwards everyone would be asking "How's Jane?" and I remember feeling resentful. Very few people said "How are you?" and I was hurting very much. You're forced to be strong when you don't want to be.'

'I had the health visitor and the doctors because of having another child and people ask the mum how she feels. But my

husband had to go back to work and people there pushed it away.'

'I went back to work the week after. There was no pressure to but it seemed the right time. Before then I called in at five one night so I could see people as they came out and they wouldn't be under any pressure to stop and talk. But people generally found it difficult to come to terms with it and it was a bit awkward. They seemed surprised I hadn't gone to pieces and they were pleased to see that but they were only supportive so long as I didn't bring it up in conversation. The real problem is finding someone to talk to. One or two were interested enough and then others would join in. As time wore on people were able to talk more easily.'

Men may find it hard to ask for help and can end up feeling very isolated and unable to let go of the sorrow built up inside. The Foundation for the Study of Infant Deaths has a helpful leaflet especially for fathers which recommends that every bereaved father finds someone to talk to – a relative, a friend, a doctor, a minister, a professional counsellor or another father who has experienced the death of a child. The Foundation may well be able to put you in touch with someone.

It's a mistake to think that men – even if they can cry and show emotion – will necessarily be able to grieve in the same way as women. There's so much history and culture bound up with the roles and expectations of fathers and mothers that reactions are almost bound to be different. If a father suppresses his own grief he may become irritable or unreasonably angry or may just appear cold and uncaring.

Returning to work, for either parent, can be a distraction, but if the mother is left at home the father will always have to make a transition from the workplace to the place of grief and that can be difficult. A leaflet produced by The Compassionate Friends (*A Father's Grief*) is very helpful in exploring these situations and the emotions experienced by bereaved fathers.

Just as people grieve in different ways, they heal at different rates and it's not hard to see how this can cause extreme tensions within a relationship.

Couples and Relationships

Cot death can have a devastating effect on a couple's relationship. Partners may find it difficult to talk to each other, to show physical affection or to agree about anything. The one may accuse the other of coldness (because he or she isn't tearful) or self-indulgence (because he or she is tearful or wants to talk endlessly about the baby). Or the partners may be so absorbed in their own grief that they can't reach out and help each other. Sex, a holiday, a meal out, making plans or just chatting over the day's events – any of the things which help to bind couples together – may seem impossible, inappropriate or even wrong. Many relationships will flounder under such a strain.

'He only talks about it very occasionally and he never instigates it. It's extremely hard and I wish he would talk. I'm sure that's what causes the arguments between us. I know men aren't very chatty but he doesn't tell the people he works with and gets annoyed if I mention it in front of them. When we were having our next baby he didn't want us to go on the CONI programme. His attitude is "what would be would be" and he was convinced it wouldn't happen again.'

The key seems to be not to expect too much of each other and to acknowledge that different people have different ways of reacting and coping. Talking to each other, hugging each other and being patient are all crucial.

'You hear of couples who split up over it and I know of one couple who are just tearing each other apart. He would not talk about it and after about three or four weeks he was telling her to pull herself together. Everybody grieves differently and, yes, there were times when I had to go off for a walk alone and other times Jane had to go off but we pulled together. To be honest we got the best support from each other. We were both strong for each other.'

Siblings

Sometimes older children are in the house or even in the room when their younger brother or sister is discovered dead. They may hear their parents' cries or they may witness desperate attempts to resuscitate the baby. In some cases an older child is the first to find the baby dead.

Children react in very different ways to these events, depending not only on their age but their personality and any part they feel they may have played in the tragedy. It is not uncommon for children to become very quiet and withdrawn, to regress to bed-wetting or thumb sucking and to change their behaviour at school – becoming aggressive or unusually silly, for example. Many children simply won't understand what has happened and may feel they are to blame. Children don't necessarily think logically.

There are many ways that children can be encouraged to come to terms with what has happened. Acting out their feelings, painting pictures, asking questions and sharing remembrances such as photographs will all help to draw out any anxieties, fears or concerns they may have. They may fear, for example, that they too will die and young children will invariably have difficulty understanding what death really means. A child under the age of five, for example, is unlikely to understand that death is forever and may ask when their younger brother or sister is coming back.

'It was very difficult because Luke was four or five at the time and he was very confused. He wasn't certain why things were happening. We answered all his questions and it was coming up to Christmas so you just have to make the effort. We tried to make things as normal as we could. But when he was in bed it was very difficult to concentrate and someone just had to say something – anything – and we might burst into tears.'

'We had to decide whether to involve our five year old in the funeral or not, so we just took it from her – she made the decision and she also had the chance to see her at the undertakers. She gave her some toys and said "Doesn't she look happy". Some people felt it wasn't right but I think she probably had less problems as a result.'

'When we had our next baby our elder daughter started having stomach problems and she asked us "Is this baby going to die too?" We had to be honest that we couldn't say definitely. But she had the support of a very good teacher and she later took part in a survey of siblings which gave us the chance to talk about it again. More recently she started crying when we were talking about Lucy but this helped us to share our feelings.'

'We actually got wonderful support from our elder daughter. It was strange but a day or so afterwards she said "Is it teatime yet?" You just fall into an oblivion but she made us realise we had to get on and do things.'

When speaking to bereaved siblings it's important to acknowledge their loss (because they have lost someone as well), to be honest, to answer questions truthfully and to explain things in a language they can understand. If you are a friend of the family, a playgroup leader or a teacher, or if your own child plays with these children, then you may have a very important part to play in listening and supporting. It's possible bereaved children may act differently and reveal their feelings more when they are away from the home which is so full of grief and memories and where they are very conscious of their parents' sorrow. If you are in this situation and you would welcome individual advice, you can call the Cot Death Helpline on 0171 235 1721. Again, the Foundation for the Study of Infant Deaths produces a helpful leaflet specifically about grief in bereaved children, as does the Children's Liver Disease Foundation (see Chapter 15 for details). A further leaflet for teachers, *When a child in your school is bereaved*, is available from The Compassionate Friends.

It's easy for parents who have suffered a cot death to become overprotective of their other children. They may also lose all confidence in themselves as parents and feel they can't cope with the caring and responsibility.

Having Another Baby

The decision whether or not to have another baby will be hard for some couples. Parents may be terrified the same thing will happen again or they may feel they are trying to replace the irreplaceable. For this reason, the Foundation for the Study of Infant Deaths has developed the Care of the Next Infant, or CONI, programme which is used by 83 per cent of NHS community trusts in England, Wales and Northern Ireland.

The CONI programme offers practical support including weekly visits by the health visitor, a symptom diary so that parents' can note any changes in the baby's health and weighing scales which are used daily by the parents. There are also weight charts, room thermometers and baby apnoea monitors (see Chapter 12), and parents are trained in resuscitation techniques.

'We went on the CONI programme when we had our second baby. Really it gave me things to think about, to occupy my mind, as there's an A4 sheet to fill in every day. But the monitor did keep going off and that was worrying.'

'The monitor went off quite a lot but it was reassuring to have. We felt by having it we were doing all we could and it makes such a difference having so much support from your doctor and health visitor which is available as part of the CONI scheme.'

'If you'd asked me two or three years ago I'd have said I'd done my grieving but I hadn't. I'd got pregnant quite quickly after Lucy died and I was so concerned about that baby that I pushed it all to the back of my mind. It wasn't until Rachael was two and out of danger that I let myself think about it and did my real grieving with the help of a close friend. She just sat with me while I did a lot of crying, sometimes shedding tears with me, and it really helped.'

For details of local CONI programmes, contact the national organiser (see Chapter 15).

Questions and Answers for Friends of Bereaved Parents

If your particular question isn't answered below or addressed in the boxes of do's and don'ts, then call the Cot Death Helpline on 0171 235 1721. The answers below have been provided by Ann Deri-Bowen of the Foundation for the Study of Infant Deaths.

Q   *Should I call at the house or just drop in a card?*

A   It is important to acknowledge that your friend or acquaintance has suffered a cot death as soon as possible. This will be easier for you if you should 'bump' into the person unexpectedly. If you are a friend you could call with a bunch of flowers or a cake and perhaps offer to do any shopping. This gives you something positive to do as well as saying how sorry you are and it helps to deal with possible embarrassment. If you are only an acquaintance you may feel more comfortable just dropping in a card. Whichever you do, refer to the baby by name.

Q   *Are there things I should avoid saying?*

A   Yes. Don't say any of the following:
   • 'You can always have another.'
   • 'You've still got one.' (if a twin dies)
   • 'He was so young you hardly got to know him.'
   • 'At least you still have other children.'
   • 'God always takes the good ones.'
   • 'The good always die young.'
   • 'I know exactly how you feel.'
   • 'It's lucky you're young enough to have lots more babies.'
   • 'You ought to be feeling better now.'
   • 'You will soon get over it.'
   • 'You'll never get over it.'

Q   *We met through antenatal classes, now I feel I will just be a constant reminder to her of what she's lost. What should I do for the best?*

A   It's true that the bereaved parents may always use the growth and development of your child to try to imagine what their child would be like. But some parents like this reminder and would do the 'imagining' anyway. Contact the parents immediately to say how sorry you are. Then try to keep in contact as often as you would have before the baby died. It's inevitable things will change if the parent goes back to work and if you only had daytime contact before then you will probably drift apart. But parents do like to continue to talk for a long time about the baby that died and you may be one of the few people who knew the baby and you may share some very important memories.

Q *I've just had a baby myself. If I visit should I leave the baby at home?*

A On the first visit to see your friend, it may be easier for you if you don't have the distractions of your baby, so you can give your friend some time and really listen to her. You may also become distressed and this time can be for you and your friend. Much will depend on your friendship and how the friend feels as to when you meet up and have the baby with you. If you find it hard to leave the baby with someone then ask your friend how she feels about you bringing him with you.

Q *If I visit them will they want to talk about it or should I talk about other things?*

A It is very important to say how sorry you are that the baby has died and to ask how the parents are feeling and be prepared for their response. They may well want to discuss the experience in great depth or they may want a 'break' from thinking about it for a while. You can take your cue from them. Certainly use the baby's name. They may be very upset and angry about some things; they may be bewildered. This could be very hard and as a friend you may feel inadequate: it's difficult when you haven't got any answers and very demanding when you have to sit alongside someone in distress and listen carefully to what they're saying.

Q   *What can I really do to help?*

A   Doing mundane things like washing, cooking and shopping can be difficult for bereaved parents. You could offer to shop or cook just to take away the burden of these household chores. Sometimes though it is better to offer your company or transport to encourage your friend to go shopping. Or you could just offer your company in their own home as well as inviting them over for supper, or just tea or coffee. It may be a long time before they feel they want to be involved in going out more formally, but some people find it easier to share a drink in the local and meet people again gradually. Always ask – they can always say that they are not ready to go out. Don't make assumptions. What is really important is that the support you offer, however small, is constant for many months after the baby's death. Some parents feel very abandoned about three months after the death – phones stop ringing and friends stop calling. A card, telephone call or some other kind of acknowledgement at anniversary times is also very much appreciated.

Chapter Fourteen

JUST FOR GRANDPARENTS

Becoming a grandparent is exciting. Whether it's your first or your tenth, each new grandchild extends your world and brings a joy which many grandparents say they had never anticipated. At the same time, particularly if you are a grandmother, you may feel for your daughter or daughter-in-law. You want to help, to offer your support and the benefit of your experience. These feelings are natural and commendable – after all, that's how wisdom is passed on and traditions inherited. Many new mothers have been eternally grateful to older women who have gently explained how to position a baby for breastfeeding, how to help bring up wind and how not to panic in those early days! Babies are babies and some things never change.

But other things do and expert advice regarding the sleeping position of babies has definitely changed since the 1960s and 1970s when many of today's grandmothers will have had their children. Parents today are urged – on the basis of overwhelming evidence – to place their babies to sleep on their backs or sides, but **not** on their tummies. This may go against the grain for many grandparents who have reared two, three or four healthy babies who slept through the night every night on their tummies, with never a hint of colic. Common sense may tell you babies are more comfortable like that and you may be able to point to hundreds of mothers who did the same as you, with no cot deaths among them. But the facts do not support the idea that putting babies to sleep on their tummies is best.

The facts are that:

◇ Babies who sleep on their tummies are between three and eight times more likely to die of cot death than babies who sleep on their backs.
◇ Sleeping on the side also poses a risk as the baby may roll onto his or her front.
◇ There's no evidence that sleeping face up makes it more likely a baby will inhale vomit and choke on it.

Chapter 4 contains more details of the way researchers have arrived at these conclusions. There are a few babies who may benefit from sleeping on their tummies – including some premature babies – but doctors will always give specific advice to the parents about this. Basically, if new parents aren't told to put their baby to sleep on his tummy then he should sleep on his back.

Other Recommendations

New parents are also advised to:

◇ Stop smoking and create a smoke-free zone around the baby (see Chapter 6).
◇ Use only sheets and blankets – not duvets, baby nests or sheepskins (see Chapters 5 and 12).
◇ Make sure the baby doesn't get too hot – by watching the room temperature and adjusting the amount of bedding accordingly and by removing hats and extra clothes when coming in from outdoors (see Chapter 12).
◇ Have the baby's basket or cot in their bedroom for the first six months (see Chapter 8).

Any or all of these recommendations has the potential to cause conflict between the generations simply because everyone evolves their own philosophy of childcare. The bywords for a happy start to your relationship with this new family are respect and restraint.

Respect

However long you have waited for this grandchild or however much you have looked forward to his arrival, it's the new parents who have responsibility for his safety and well-being. Their views and wishes are central and deserve respect. New parents can seem particularly fussy and anxious, but you will win their trust and affection if, for example, you respect their wishes to have a smoke-free house and only smoke in the garden. If you want to be left in charge of the baby from time to time then you need to show you're willing to follow their lead.

Restraint

New parents may be very sensitive to what you see as helpful advice but which they perceive as criticism, so a bit of tongue-biting won't go amiss in the first few weeks. As time goes on and the new parents become more confident they probably won't feel so sensitive and may be more willing to discuss alternative practices. Restraint may also be useful in situations where the new parents are confident of their own opinions but are afraid of alienating you – they need your practical help at this difficult and busy time and the last thing they want is an argument.

Hints for Giving Advice

◇ If possible, wait until you are asked for advice. Or you could offer in a general way – 'You seem as though you're coping really well but if I can help at all please do ask.'

◇ If you feel the baby is at risk in some way – for example, if you feel he is going to get cold because too few blankets are being used – you could ask what advice the parents have had about this and see if they are following any specific guidance or would welcome your help – 'What did they tell you about . . . ?'.

◇ Remember women can be very sensitive in the first few days after they have given birth because of the extreme hormone changes they are experiencing.

◇ Be prepared to listen to the new parents' views.

◇ Introduce 'advice' in the context of a discussion about 'the way things used to be'. This leaves the door open for the new parents to tell you what advice they've been given and have chosen to follow and no-one feels criticised.

◇ Don't be offended if your advice isn't taken.

Chapter Fifteen

SOURCES OF HELP

The Foundation for the Study of Infant Deaths (FSID)
14 Halkin Street
London SW1X 7DP
General enquiries Tel: 0171 235 0965, Fax: 0171 823 1986
24-hour Cot Death Helpline Tel: 0171 235 1721
Appeals Tel: 0171 823 2216
e-mail fsid@dial.pipex.com

Mrs Alison Waite
National CONI Organiser
Room C1, Stephenson Unit
University of Sheffield
Western Bank
Sheffield S10 2TH
Tel: 0114 276 6452

Scottish Cot Death Trust
Royal Hospital for Sick Children
Yorkhill
Glasgow G3 8SJ
General enquiries Tel: 0141 357 3946

Irish Sudden Infant Death Association
Carmichael House
4 North Brunswick Street
Dublin 7
General enquiries Tel: 00 353 1 8726 199
Cot Death Helpline Tel: 00 353 1 8747 007

Compassionate Friends
53 North Street
Bristol BS3 1EN
Tel: 0117 953 9639
Parents who've lost a child and are willing to support and befriend parents in a similar position.

Cruse Bereavement Care
126 Sheen Road
Richmond
Surrey TW9 1UR
Tel: 0181 940 4818
Cruse Bereavement Helpline Tel: 0181 332 7227,
open 9.30am–5pm, Monday–Friday

Stillbirth and Neonatal Death Society (SANDS)
28 Portland Place
London W1N 4DE
Tel: 0171 436 5881

Children's Liver Disease Foundation
Ist Floor
138 Digbeth
Birmingham B5 6DR
Tel: 0121 643 7282
Free leaflet on 'Children and Bereavement'. Please send sae.

Relate – National Marriage Guidance Council
Herbert Gray College
Little Church Street
Rugby
Warwickshire CV21 3AP
Tel: 01788 573241, or see under RELATE or Marriage
Guidance in the local telephone book.
*Confidential counselling for couples or individual partners
with relationship problems.*

Association of Burial Authorities
139 Kensington High Street
London W8 6SX
Tel: 0171 937 0052

For general information on smoking:

Action on Smoking and Health (ASH)
109 Gloucester Place
London W1H 4EJ
General enquiries Tel: 0171 935 3519

For help to stop smoking:

QUIT
Victory House
170 Tottenham Court Road
London W1P 0HA
Helpline Tel: 0171 487 3000

For details of Baby Check *booklet with or without
thermometer:*

Baby Check
PO Box 324, Wroxham
Norwich NR12 8EQ

For details of the St John Ambulance Babies and Children Lifesaver course, contact your local branch of St John Ambulance or write to:

St John Ambulance
1 Grosvenor Crescent
London SW1X 7EF

Organisations providing information and/or support for lone parents include:

Gingerbread
49 Wellington Street
London WC2E 7BN
Tel: 0171 240 0953

National Council for One Parent Families
255 Kentish Town Road
London NW5 2LX
Tel: 0171 267 1361

'It's such simple advice and it's so worth bothering with.
The last thing I expected was my baby would die.
I just wish I'd known then what I know now.'

INDEX